TRANZLATY

Language is for everyone

言語はすべての人のためのもの

The Call of the Wild

野生の呼び声

Jack London

English / 日本語

Into the Primitive
原始の世界へ

Buck did not read the newspapers.
バックは新聞を読まなかった

Had he read the newspapers he would have known trouble was brewing.
もし彼が新聞を読んでいたら、問題が起こりつつあることを知っていただろう

There was trouble not alone for himself, but for every tidewater dog.
問題は彼自身だけではなく、すべての海水犬に起こった

Every dog strong of muscle and with warm, long hair was going to be in trouble.
筋肉が強く、暖かくて長い毛を持つ犬は皆、困ったことになるだろう

From Puget Bay to San Diego no dog could escape what was coming.
ピュージェット湾からサンディエゴまで、どんな犬もこれから起こることを逃れることはできない

Men, groping in the Arctic darkness, had found a yellow metal.
男たちは北極の暗闇の中を手探りで探し、黄色い金属を発見した

Steamship and transportation companies were chasing the discovery.
蒸気船会社と運送会社がこの発見を追いかけていた

Thousands of men were rushing into the Northland.
何千人もの男たちが北の地へ押し寄せていた

These men wanted dogs, and the dogs they wanted were heavy dogs.
この男たちは犬を欲しがっていたが、彼らが欲しかった犬は大型犬だった

Dogs with strong muscles by which to toil.
労働に耐えられる強い筋肉を持つ犬

Dogs with furry coats to protect them from the frost.

霜から身を守るために毛皮で覆われた犬

Buck lived at a big house in the sun-kissed Santa Clara Valley.
バックは太陽が降り注ぐサンタクララバレーの大きな家に住んでいました

Judge Miller's place, his house was called.
ミラー判事の所、彼の家と呼ばれていました

His house stood back from the road, half hidden among the trees.
彼の家は道路から少し離れたところに建っていて、木々の間に半分隠れていた

One could get glimpses of the wide veranda running around the house.
家の周囲を巡る広いベランダを垣間見ることができました

The house was approached by graveled driveways.
家へは砂利敷きの私道を通って行くことができました

The paths wound about through wide-spreading lawns.
小道は広々とした芝生の間を曲がりくねって通っていた

Overhead were the interlacing boughs of tall poplars.
頭上には背の高いポプラの枝が絡み合っていた

At the rear of the house things were on even more spacious.
家の裏側はさらに広々としていました

There were great stables, where a dozen grooms were chatting
大きな厩舎があり、そこでは12人の厩務員が雑談していた

There were rows of vine-clad servants' cottages
ブドウの木に覆われた使用人の小屋が並んでいた

And there was an endless and orderly array of outhouses
そして、そこには整然と並んだ屋外トイレが無数にありました

Long grape arbors, green pastures, orchards, and berry patches.
長いブドウ棚、緑の牧草地、果樹園、ベリー畑

Then there was the pumping plant for the artesian well.
それから自噴井戸用のポンプ場もありました

And there was the big cement tank filled with water.
そしてそこには水が満たされた大きなセメントタンクが
ありました

Here Judge Miller's boys took their morning plunge.
ここでミラー判事の息子たちが朝のひとときを過ごしま
した

And they cooled down there in the hot afternoon too.
そして暑い午後もそこで涼しく過ごしました

And over this great domain, Buck was the one who ruled all
of it.
そして、この広大な領土のすべてを支配していたのはバ
ックでした

Buck was born on this land and lived here all his four years.
バックはこの土地で生まれ、4年間をここで暮らしまし
た

There were indeed other dogs, but they did not truly matter.
確かに他の犬もいたが、それらは本当に問題ではなかっ
た

Other dogs were expected in a place as vast as this one.
これほど広大な場所には、他の犬もいるはずだ

These dogs came and went, or lived inside the busy kennels.
これらの犬たちは出入りしたり、忙しい犬舎の中で暮ら
したりしていました

Some dogs lived hidden in the house, like Toots and Ysabel
did.
トゥーツやイザベルのように、家の中に隠れて暮らす犬
もいました

Toots was a Japanese pug, Ysabel a Mexican hairless dog.
トゥーツは日本のパグで、イザベルはメキシコの無毛犬
でした

These strange creatures rarely stepped outside the house.
これらの奇妙な生き物たちはめったに家の外に出ません
でした

They did not touch the ground, nor sniff the open air outside.

彼らは地面に触れることも、外の空気を嗅ぐこともしませんでした

There were also the fox terriers, at least twenty in number.

フォックステリアも少なくとも20匹はいました

These terriers barked fiercely at Toots and Ysabel indoors.

このテリア犬たちは家の中でトゥーツとイザベルに向かって激しく吠えました

Toots and Ysabel stayed behind windows, safe from harm.

トゥーツとイザベルは窓の後ろに留まり、危害を受けないようにしました

They were guarded by housemaids with brooms and mops.

彼らはほうきとモップを持ったメイドたちによって守られていました

But Buck was no house-dog, and he was no kennel-dog either.

しかし、バックは家犬ではなかったし、犬小屋犬でもなかった

The entire property belonged to Buck as his rightful realm.

その全財産はバックの正当な領土であった

Buck swam in the tank or went hunting with the Judge's sons.

バックは水槽で泳いだり、判事の息子たちと一緒に狩りに出かけたりしました

He walked with Mollie and Alice in the early or late hours.

彼は早朝や深夜にモリーとアリスと一緒に散歩した

On cold nights he lay before the library fire with the Judge.

寒い夜には、彼は判事とともに図書館の暖炉の前に横たわった

Buck gave rides to the Judge's grandsons on his strong back.

バックは力強い背中に乗って判事の孫たちを乗せて行きました

He rolled in the grass with the boys, guarding them closely.

彼は少年たちと一緒に草むらで転がり、彼らをしっかりと見守った

They ventured to the fountain and even past the berry fields.
彼らは噴水まで足を延ばし、ベリー畑を通り過ぎました
Among the fox terriers, Buck walked with royal pride always.
フォックステリアたちの間で、バックは常に王者の誇りを持って歩き回っていました
He ignored Toots and Ysabel, treating them like they were air.
彼はトゥーツとイザベルを無視し、彼らを空気のように扱いました
Buck ruled over all living creatures on Judge Miller's land.
バックはミラー判事の土地のすべての生き物を支配した
He ruled over animals, insects, birds, and even humans.
彼は動物、昆虫、鳥、そして人間さえも支配しました
Buck's father Elmo had been a huge and loyal St. Bernard.
バックの父親エルモは、大きくて忠実なセントバーナード犬でした
Elmo never left the Judge's side, and served him faithfully.
エルモは裁判官の側を決して離れず、忠実に裁判官に仕えました
Buck seemed ready to follow his father's noble example.
バックは父親の高潔な例に従うつもりのようだった
Buck was not quite as large, weighing one hundred and forty pounds.
バックはそれほど大きくなく、体重は140ポンドでした
His mother, Shep, had been a fine Scotch shepherd dog.
彼の母親のシェップは立派なスコッチ・シェパード・ドッグだった
But even at that weight, Buck walked with regal presence.
しかし、その体重であっても、バックは堂々とした存在感をもって歩いていた
This came from good food and the respect he always received.
これはおいしい食事と彼がいつも受けてきた尊敬から生まれたものでした
For four years, Buck had lived like a spoiled nobleman.

バックは4年間、甘やかされた貴族のような暮らしをしていた

He was proud of himself, and even slightly egotistical.
彼は自分に誇りを持っており、少々自己中心的でさえあった

That kind of pride was common in remote country lords.
そのような誇りは、辺鄙な田舎の領主の間では一般的でした

But Buck saved himself from becoming pampered house-dog.
しかし、バックは甘やかされた飼い犬になることを免れた

He stayed lean and strong through hunting and exercise.
彼は狩猟と運動を通じて引き締まった体型と強靱な体型を保っていた

He loved water deeply, like people who bathe in cold lakes.
彼は、冷たい湖で水浴びをする人々のように、水を深く愛していました

This love for water kept Buck strong, and very healthy.
水に対するこの愛情のおかげで、バックは強く、非常に健康でした

This was the dog Buck had become in the fall of 1897.
これは、1897 年の秋にバックが変身した犬です

When the Klondike strike pulled men to the frozen North.
クロンダイクの襲撃により、人々は凍てつく北の地へと引き寄せられた

People rushed from all over the world into the cold land.
人々は世界中から寒い土地へと押し寄せました

Buck, however, did not read the papers, nor understand news.
しかし、バックは新聞を読まなかったし、ニュースも理解していなかった

He did not know Manuel was a bad man to be around.
彼はマヌエルが一緒にいて悪い男だとは知らなかった

Manuel, who helped in the garden, had a deep problem.

庭仕事を手伝っていたマヌエルは深刻な問題を抱えていた

Manuel was addicted to gambling in the Chinese lottery.
マヌエルは中国の宝くじギャンブルに夢中だった

He also believed strongly in a fixed system for winning.
彼はまた、勝利のための固定されたシステムを強く信じていた

That belief made his failure certain and unavoidable.
その信念により、彼の失敗は確実かつ避けられないものとなった

Playing a system demands money, which Manuel lacked.
システムをプレイするにはお金が必要ですが、マヌエルにはそれがありませんでした

His pay barely supported his wife and many children.
彼の給料は妻と多くの子供たちを養うのにやっとのことでした

On the night Manuel betrayed Buck, things were normal.
マヌエルがバックを裏切った夜、物事は普通だった

The Judge was at a Raisin Growers' Association meeting.
裁判官はレーズン栽培者協会の会合に出席していた

The Judge's sons were busy forming an athletic club then.
当時、判事の息子たちは運動クラブの設立に忙しかった

No one saw Manuel and Buck leaving through the orchard.
マヌエルとバックが果樹園を通って去っていくのを見た人は誰もいなかった

Buck thought this walk was just a simple nighttime stroll.
バックはこの散歩は単なる夜間の散歩だと思っていた

They met only one man at the flag station, in College Park.
彼らはカレッジパークのフラッグステーションでたった一人の男に出会った

That man spoke to Manuel, and they exchanged money.
その男はマヌエルに話しかけ、二人はお金を交換した

"Wrap up the goods before you deliver them," he suggested.
「商品を配達する前に包んでください」と彼は提案した

The man's voice was rough and impatient as he spoke.
その男は話すとき、荒々しく、いらだたしい声だった

Manuel carefully tied a thick rope around Buck's neck.
マヌエルはバックの首に太いロープを慎重に巻き付けた

"Twist the rope, and you'll choke him plenty"
「ロープをねじれば、十分に絞められる」

The stranger gave a grunt, showing he understood well.
その見知らぬ男はうなり声をあげ、よく理解したことを示した

Buck accepted the rope with calm and quiet dignity that day.
その日、バックは落ち着いて静かに威厳をもってロープを受け取った

It was an unusual act, but Buck trusted the men he knew.
それは珍しい行為だったが、バックは自分が知っている男たちを信頼していた

He believed their wisdom went far beyond his own thinking.
彼らの知恵は彼自身の考えをはるかに超えていると彼は信じていた

But then the rope was handed to the hands of the stranger.
しかし、その後、ロープは見知らぬ人の手に渡されました

Buck gave a low growl that warned with quiet menace.
バックは静かな威嚇で警告する低い唸り声を上げた

He was proud and commanding, and meant to show his displeasure.
彼は傲慢で命令口調で、不快感を示したかったのだ

Buck believed his warning would be understood as an order.
バックは彼の警告が命令として理解されるだろうと信じていた

To his shock, the rope tightened fast around his thick neck.
驚いたことに、ロープが彼の太い首に急にきつく締まりました

His air was cut off and he began to fight in a sudden rage.
彼の呼吸は止められ、突然の激怒で彼は戦い始めた

He sprang at the man, who quickly met Buck in mid-air.
バックは男に向かって飛びかかったが、男はすぐに空中でバックと出会った

The man grabbed Buck's throat and skillfully twisted him in the air.

男はバックの喉を掴み、巧みに空中でひねり上げた

Buck was thrown down hard, landing flat on his back.

バックは激しく投げ出され、背中から地面に倒れた

The rope now choked him cruelly while he kicked wildly.

彼が激しく足を蹴る間、ロープは残酷に彼の首を締め付けた

His tongue fell out, his chest heaved, but gained no breath.

舌は出てきて、胸は上下に動いたが、呼吸はできなかった

He had never been treated with such violence in his life.

彼は生涯でこれほどの暴力を受けたことはなかった

He had also never been filled with such deep fury before.

彼はこれまでこれほど激しい怒りに駆られたことはなかった

But Buck's power faded, and his eyes turned glassy.

しかし、バックの力は弱まり、彼の目は生気を失った

He passed out just as a train was flagged down nearby.

ちょうど近くで列車が止まったとき、彼は気を失った

Then the two men tossed him into the baggage car quickly.

それから二人の男は彼を手早く荷物車に放り込んだ

The next thing Buck felt was pain in his swollen tongue.

次にバックが感じたのは腫れた舌の痛みだった

He was moving in a shaking cart, only dimly conscious.

彼はぼんやりとした意識で、揺れるカートに乗って移動していた

The sharp scream of a train whistle told Buck his location.

鋭い汽笛の音がバックに自分の居場所を知らせた

He had often ridden with the Judge and knew the feeling.

彼は判事と一緒に何度も乗馬したことがあり、その気持ちはよく分かっていた

It was the unique jolt of traveling in a baggage car again.

それは再び荷物車で旅行するという独特の衝撃でした

Buck opened his eyes, and his gaze burned with rage.

バックは目を開けたそして、その視線は怒りで燃えていた

This was the anger of a proud king taken from his throne.
これは王位を奪われた傲慢な王の怒りだった

A man reached to grab him, but Buck struck first instead.
男は彼をつかもうとしたが、代わりにバックが先に攻撃した

He sank his teeth into the man's hand and held tightly.
彼は男の手に歯を食い込ませ、しっかりと握りしめた

He did not let go until he blacked out a second time.
彼は二度目に気を失うまで手を離さなかった

"Yep, has fits," the man muttered to the baggageman.
「ああ、発作を起こすんだ」男は荷物係にぶつぶつ言った

The baggageman had heard the struggle and come near.
荷物係は争っているのを聞きつけて近づいてきた

"I'm taking him to 'Frisco for the boss," the man explained.
「ボスのために彼をフリスコに連れて行くんだ」と男は説明した

"There's a fine dog-doctor there who says he can cure them."
「そこには、彼らを治せると言っている優秀な犬の医者がいます」

Later that night the man gave his own full account.
その夜遅く、その男は自ら詳しく話した

He spoke from a shed behind a saloon on the docks.
彼は港の酒場の裏の小屋から話した

"All I was given was fifty dollars," he complained to the saloon man.
「私に渡されたのはたった50ドルだけだった」と彼は酒場の主人に不満を漏らした

"I wouldn't do it again, not even for a thousand in cold cash."
「たとえ1000ドルの現金をもらっても、二度とそんなことはしません」

His right hand was tightly wrapped in a bloody cloth.
彼の右手は血まみれの布でしっかりと巻かれていた

His trouser leg was torn wide open from knee to foot.
彼のズボンの脚は膝から足まで大きく引き裂かれていた

"How much did the other mug get paid?" asked the saloon man.
「もう一人の馬鹿はいくらもらったんだ？」酒場の主人が尋ねた

"A hundred," the man replied, "he wouldn't take a cent less."
「100ドルです」と男は答えた「それ以下では一銭も受け取りません」

"That comes to a hundred and fifty," the saloon man said.
「合計150になります」と酒場の主人は言った

"And he's worth it all, or I'm no better than a blockhead."
「そして彼はその全てに値するそうでなければ私はただの愚か者だ」

The man opened the wrappings to examine his hand.
男は自分の手を調べるために包みを開けた

The hand was badly torn and crusted in dried blood.
その手はひどく裂けており、乾いた血で固まっていた

"If I don't get the hydrophobia..." he began to say.
「恐水症にならなければ…」と彼は言い始めた

"It'll be because you were born to hang," came a laugh.
「それはあなたがぶら下がるために生まれてきたからでしょう」と笑い声が聞こえた

"Come help me out before you get going," he was asked.
「出発する前に手伝ってくれないか」と彼は頼まれた

Buck was in a daze from the pain in his tongue and throat.
バックは舌と喉の痛みでぼうっとしていた

He was half-strangled, and could barely stand upright.
彼は半分絞め殺され、ほとんどまっすぐに立つこともできなかった

Still, Buck tried to face the men who had hurt him so.
それでも、バックは自分をここまで傷つけた男たちと向き合おうとした

But they threw him down and choked him once again.
しかし彼らは再び彼を投げ倒し、首を絞めました

Only then could they saw off his heavy brass collar.
そうして初めて、彼らは彼の重い真鍮の首輪を切り落とすことができた

They removed the rope and shoved him into a crate.
彼らはロープを外して彼を木箱に押し込んだ

The crate was small and shaped like a rough iron cage.
その木箱は小さくて、粗雑な鉄の檻のような形をしていた

Buck lay there all night, filled with wrath and wounded pride.
バックは怒りと傷ついたプライドに満たされ、一晩中そこに横たわっていた

He could not begin to understand what was happening to him.
彼は自分に何が起こっているのか全く理解できなかった

Why were these strange men keeping him in this small crate?
なぜこの見知らぬ男たちは彼をこの小さな木箱の中に閉じ込めていたのでしょうか?

What did they want with him, and why this cruel captivity?
彼らは彼に何を望んでいたのか、そしてなぜこのような残酷な監禁をしていたのか?

He felt a dark pressure; a sense of disaster drawing closer.
彼は暗いプレッシャーを感じ、災難が近づいていると感じた

It was a vague fear, but it settled heavily on his spirit.
それは漠然とした恐怖だったが、彼の心に重くのしかかった

Several times he jumped up when the shed door rattled.
小屋のドアがガタガタと音を立てると、彼は何度か飛び上がった

He expected the Judge or the boys to appear and rescue him.
彼は裁判官か少年たちが現れて彼を救ってくれることを期待していた

But only the saloon-keeper's fat face peeked inside each time.

しかし、そのたびに中を覗くのは酒場主人の太った顔だけだった

The man's face was lit by the dim glow of a tallow candle.
男の顔は獣脂ろうそくのぼんやりとした光で照らされていた

Each time, Buck's joyful bark changed to a low, angry growl.
そのたびに、バックの喜びに満ちた吠え声は、低く怒った唸り声に変わった

The saloon-keeper left him alone for the night in the crate
酒場の主人は彼を一晩中箱の中に残していった

But when he awoke in the morning more men were coming.
しかし、朝目覚めると、さらに多くの男たちがやって来ていた

Four men came and gingerly picked up the crate without a word.
4人の男がやって来て、何も言わずにそっと木箱を持ち上げました

Buck knew at once the situation he found himself in.
バックはすぐに自分が置かれた状況を悟った

They were further tormentors that he had to fight and fear.
彼らは彼が戦って恐れなければならなかったさらなる拷問者でした

These men looked wicked, ragged, and very badly groomed.
これらの男たちは邪悪で、ぼろぼろの服を着ており、身だしなみもひどく悪そうに見えました

Buck snarled and lunged at them fiercely through the bars.
バックは唸り声をあげ、格子越しに激しく彼らに突進した

They just laughed and jabbed at him with long wooden sticks.
彼らはただ笑って、長い木の棒で彼を突いた

Buck bit at the sticks, then realized that was what they liked.
バックは棒を噛み、それが彼らが好きなものだと気づきました

So he lay down quietly, sullen and burning with quiet rage.

そこで彼は静かに横たわり、不機嫌になり、静かな怒り
に燃えていた

They lifted the crate into a wagon and drove away with him.
彼らは木箱を荷馬車に積み込み、彼を連れて走り去った

The crate, with Buck locked inside, changed hands often.
バックが中に閉じ込められていた木箱は、頻繁に所有者
が変わった.

Express office clerks took charge and handled him briefly.
急行便の事務員が担当し、簡単に対応してくれました

Then another wagon carried Buck across the noisy town.
それから別の荷馬車がバックを騒がしい町の向こうへ運
んだ

A truck took him with boxes and parcels onto a ferry boat.
トラックが彼を箱や小包とともにフェリー船に乗せた

After crossing, the truck unloaded him at a rail depot.
国境を越えた後、トラックは彼を鉄道駅で降ろした

At last, Buck was placed inside a waiting express car.
ついに、バックは待機していた急行車両に乗せられまし
た

For two days and nights, trains pulled the express car away.
二日二晩にわたって、列車が急行車両を牽引しました

**Buck neither ate nor drank during the whole painful
journey.**
バックは苦しい旅の間中、食べることも飲むこともしな
かった

**When the express messengers tried to approach him, he
growled.**
急使たちが彼に近づこうとしたとき、彼はうなり声をあ
げた

They responded by mocking him and teasing him cruelly.
彼らは彼を嘲笑し、残酷にからかって応じた

Buck threw himself at the bars, foaming and shaking
バックは泡を吹きながら震えながら鉄格子に飛びついた

**they laughed loudly, and taunted him like schoolyard
bullies.**

彼らは大声で笑い、まるで学校のいじめっ子のように彼をからかった

They barked like fake dogs and flapped their arms.
彼らは偽の犬のように吠え、腕をバタバタさせました

They even crowed like roosters just to upset him more.
彼らは彼をさらに怒らせるために、雄鶏のように鳴きさえしました

It was foolish behavior, and Buck knew it was ridiculous.
それは愚かな行為であり、バックはそれが馬鹿げていることを知っていた

But that only deepened his sense of outrage and shame.
しかし、それによって彼の怒りと恥の意識は深まるばかりだった

He was not bothered much by hunger during the trip.
彼は旅行中、空腹にあまり悩まされることはなかった

But thirst brought sharp pain and unbearable suffering.
しかし、渇きは激しい痛みと耐え難い苦しみをもたらしました

His dry, inflamed throat and tongue burned with heat.
彼の乾燥して炎症を起こした喉と舌は熱く燃えるように痛んだ

This pain fed the fever rising within his proud body.
この痛みは彼の誇り高き体の中で高まる熱を増大させた

Buck was thankful for one single thing during this trial.
バックはこの裁判中、ただ一つのことに感謝していた

The rope had been removed from around his thick neck.
彼の太い首に巻かれていたロープは外されていた

The rope had given those men an unfair and cruel advantage.
ロープは彼らに不公平かつ残酷な優位性を与えていた

Now the rope was gone, and Buck swore it would never return.
今やロープは消え去っており、バックはそれが二度と戻らないと誓った

He resolved no rope would ever go around his neck again.
彼は二度と自分の首にロープを巻かないことを決意した

For two long days and nights, he suffered without food.
彼は二日間と二晩、食べ物もなく苦しみ続けた

And in those hours, he built up an enormous rage inside.
そして、その数時間の間に、彼は心の中に大きな怒りを蓄積していった

His eyes turned bloodshot and wild from constant anger.
彼の目は絶え間ない怒りのせいで充血し狂ったようになっていた

He was no longer Buck, but a demon with snapping jaws.
彼はもうバックではなく、パクパクと顎を鳴らす悪魔だった

Even the Judge would not have known this mad creature.
裁判官でさえこの狂った生き物を知らなかっただろう

The express messengers sighed in relief when they reached Seattle
速達の使者たちはシアトルに到着すると安堵のため息をついた

Four men lifted the crate and brought it to a back yard.
4人の男が木箱を持ち上げて裏庭に運んだ

The yard was small, surrounded by high and solid walls.
庭は狭く、高くて頑丈な壁に囲まれていました

A big man stepped out in a sagging red sweater shirt.
だぶだぶの赤いセーターシャツを着た大男が出てきた

He signed the delivery book with a thick and bold hand.
彼は配達記録簿に太くて力強い手書きで署名した

Buck sensed at once that this man was his next tormentor.
バックはすぐにこの男が自分を苦しめる次の相手だと察した

He lunged violently at the bars, eyes red with fury.
彼は怒りで目を真っ赤にして、鉄格子に向かって激しく突進した

The man just smiled darkly and went to fetch a hatchet.
男は暗い笑みを浮かべると、斧を取りに行きました

He also brought a club in his thick and strong right hand.
彼はまた、分厚く力強い右手に棍棒を持っていた

"You going to take him out now?" the driver asked, concerned.
「今から彼を連れ出すつもりですか？」運転手は心配そうに尋ねた

"Sure," said the man, jamming the hatchet into the crate as a lever.
「もちろんだ」男は梃子代わりに斧を木箱に押し込みながら言った

The four men scattered instantly, jumping up onto the yard wall.
4人の男たちはすぐに散り散りになり、庭の壁の上に飛び上がった

From their safe spots above, they waited to watch the spectacle.
彼らは上の安全な場所から、その光景を眺めるのを待っていた

Buck lunged at the splintered wood, biting and shaking fiercely.
バックは砕けた木に突進し、激しく噛みつきながら震えていた

Each time the hatchet hit the cage), Buck was there to attack it.
斧が檻に当たるたびに、バックがそこにいて攻撃した

He growled and snapped with wild rage, eager to be set free.
彼は解放されることを切望し、激しい怒りで唸り声をあげ、噛みついた

The man outside was calm and steady, intent on his task.
外の男は落ち着いていて落ち着いており、自分の仕事に集中していた

"Right then, you red-eyed devil," he said when the hole was large.
「そうだな、この赤い目の悪魔」穴が大きくなったとき、彼はそう言った

He dropped the hatchet and took the club in his right hand.
彼は斧を落とし、右手に棍棒を取った

Buck truly looked like a devil; eyes bloodshot and blazing.

バックは本当に悪魔のように見えました目は充血して燃えていました

His coat bristled, foam frothed at his mouth, eyes glinting.
彼のコートは逆立ち、口からは泡が吹き、目はきらきらと輝いていた

He bunched his muscles and sprang straight at the red sweater.
彼は筋肉を収縮させ、真っ直ぐに赤いセーターに向かって飛びかかった

One hundred and forty pounds of fury flew at the calm man.
140ポンドの怒りが冷静な男に向かって飛び散った

Just before his jaws clamped shut, a terrible blow struck him.
顎が閉じる直前、恐ろしい一撃が彼を襲った

His teeth snapped together on nothing but air
彼の歯は空気だけでカチカチと音を立てた

a jolt of pain reverberated through his body
激しい痛みが彼の体中に響き渡った

He flipped midair and crashed down on his back and side.
彼は空中で回転し、背中と横から地面に倒れ込んだ

He had never before felt a club's blow and could not grasp it.
彼はこれまで棍棒の打撃を感じたことがなく、それを理解することができなかった

With a shrieking snarl, part bark, part scream, he leaped again.
叫び声のような、吠え声のようなうなり声とともに、彼は再び飛び上がった

Another brutal strike hit him and hurled him to the ground.
もう一度の残忍な一撃が彼を襲い、地面に叩きつけられた

This time Buck understood—it was the man's heavy club.
今度はバックは理解した——それは男の重い棍棒だったのだ

But rage blinded him, and he had no thought of retreat.

しかし、怒りのあまり彼は目が見えなくなり、撤退する
考えもなかった

Twelve times he launched himself, and twelve times he fell.
彼は12回飛び上がり、12回落ちた

**The wooden club smashed him each time with ruthless,
crushing force.**
そのたびに、木の棍棒は容赦なく、圧倒的な力で彼を打
ち砕いた

**After one fierce blow, he staggered to his feet, dazed and
slow.**
激しい一撃を受けた後、彼は茫然としてよろめきながら
ゆっくりと立ち上がった

Blood ran from his mouth, his nose, and even his ears.
彼の口、鼻、さらには耳からも血が流れ出た

His once-beautiful coat was smeared with bloody foam.
かつて美しかった彼の毛皮は血の泡で汚れていた

**Then the man stepped up and struck a wicked blow to the
nose.**
すると男が近づき、鼻にひどい一撃を加えた

The agony was sharper than anything Buck had ever felt.
その苦痛はバックがこれまで感じたことのなかったもの
よりも激しいものだった

With a roar more beast than dog, he leaped again to attack.
彼は犬というより獣のような咆哮をあげ、再び飛びかか
って攻撃した

But the man caught his lower jaw and twisted it backward.
しかし、男は彼の下顎を掴み、後ろにひねった

Buck flipped head over heels, crashing down hard again.
バックはひっくり返って、再び激しく地面に落ちた

**One final time, Buck charged at him, now barely able to
stand.**
バックは最後にもう一度、かろうじて立つことができた
状態で彼に突進した

**The man struck with expert timing, delivering the final
blow.**
男は熟練したタイミングで攻撃し、とどめを刺した

Buck collapsed in a heap, unconscious and unmoving.
バックは意識を失い、動かずに倒れてしまいました

"He's no slouch at dog-breaking, that's what I say," a man yelled.
「彼は犬の調教が下手なわけではない、それが私の意見だ」と男は叫んだ

"Druther can break the will of a hound any day of the week."
「ドゥルーザーはいつでも猟犬の意志を折ることができる」

"And twice on a Sunday!" added the driver.
「しかも日曜日には２回も！」と運転手は付け加えた

He climbed into the wagon and cracked the reins to leave.
彼は荷馬車に乗り込み、手綱を鳴らして出発した

Buck slowly regained control of his consciousness
バックはゆっくりと意識を取り戻した

but his body was still too weak and broken to move.
しかし、彼の体はまだ動くには弱りきっていて壊れていました

He lay where he had fallen, watching the red-sweatered man.
彼は倒れた場所に横たわり、赤いセーターを着た男を見つめていた

"He answers to the name of Buck," the man said, reading aloud.
「彼はバックという名で呼ばれています」男は声を出して読みながら言った

He quoted from the note sent with Buck's crate and details.
彼はバックの木箱と一緒に送られたメモから詳細を引用した

"Well, Buck, my boy," the man continued with a friendly tone,
「そうだな、バック、坊や」男は友好的な口調で続けた

"we've had our little fight, and now it's over between us."
「ちょっとした喧嘩をしたけど、もう私たちの関係は終わった」

"You've learned your place, and I've learned mine," he added.

「君は自分の立場を学んだし、私も自分の立場を学んだ」と彼は付け加えた

"Be good, and all will go well, and life will be pleasant."

「善良であれそうすればすべてはうまくいき、人生は楽しいものとなる」

"But be bad, and I'll beat the stuffing out of you, understand?"

「でも、悪いことをしたら、ぶん殴ってやるからな、分かったか？」

As he spoke, he reached out and patted Buck's sore head.

そう言いながら、彼は手を伸ばしてバックの痛む頭を軽くたたいた

Buck's hair rose at the man's touch, but he didn't resist.

男に触れられてバックの髪は逆立ったが、彼は抵抗しなかった

The man brought him water, which Buck drank in great gulps.

男は彼に水を持って来たので、バックはそれを一気に飲んだ

Then came raw meat, which Buck devoured chunk by chunk.

それから生の肉が運ばれてきて、バックはそれを一口ずつ食べ尽くした

He knew he was beaten, but he also knew he wasn't broken.

彼は自分が負けたことを知っていたが、まだ壊れていないことも知っていた

He had no chance against a man armed with a club.

棍棒で武装した男に彼に勝ち目はなかった

He had learned the truth, and he never forgot that lesson.

彼は真実を学び、その教訓を決して忘れなかった

That weapon was the beginning of law in Buck's new world.

その武器はバックの新しい世界における法の始まりでした

It was the start of a harsh, primitive order he could not deny.

それは彼が否定することのできない、過酷で原始的な秩序の始まりだった

He accepted the truth; his wild instincts were now awake.
彼は真実を受け入れた彼の野生の本能が目覚めたのだ

The world had grown harsher, but Buck faced it bravely.
世界はより厳しくなっていたが、バックは勇敢にそれに立ち向かった

He met life with new caution, cunning, and quiet strength.
彼は新たな注意深さ、狡猾さ、そして静かな強さで人生に立ち向かった

More dogs arrived, tied in ropes or crates like Buck had been.
バックと同じように、ロープや箱に縛られた犬がさらにたくさんやって来ました

Some dogs came calmly, others raged and fought like wild beasts.
落ち着いてやってくる犬もいれば、野獣のように激怒して戦う犬もいました

All of them were brought under the rule of the red-sweatered man.
彼ら全員は赤いセーターを着た男の支配下に置かれました

Each time, Buck watched and saw the same lesson unfold.
そのたびに、バックは同じ教訓が展開されるのを観察しました

The man with the club was law; a master to be obeyed.
棍棒を持った男は法律であり、従うべき主人だった

He did not need to be liked, but he had to be obeyed.
彼は好かれる必要はなかったが、従われる必要はあった

Buck never fawned or wagged like the weaker dogs did.
バックは、弱い犬たちのように媚びへつらったり尻尾を振ったりすることは決してなかった

He saw dogs that were beaten and still licked the man's hand.
彼は、殴られてもなお男の手を舐め続ける犬たちを見た

He saw one dog who would not obey or submit at all.

彼は、まったく従わない、服従しない犬を一匹見かけました

That dog fought until he was killed in the battle for control.
その犬は支配権をめぐる戦いで殺されるまで戦い続けた

Strangers would sometimes come to see the red-sweatered man.
時々、見知らぬ人が赤いセーターを着た男に会いに来ることもあった

They spoke in strange tones, pleading, bargaining, and laughing.
彼らは奇妙な口調で話し、懇願したり、交渉したり、笑ったりした

When money was exchanged, they left with one or more dogs.
お金を交換すると、彼らは一匹以上の犬を連れて帰りました

Buck wondered where these dogs went, for none ever returned.
バックはこれらの犬たちがどこへ行ったのか不思議に思った一匹も戻ってこなかったからだ

fear of the unknown filled Buck every time a strange man came
見知らぬ男が来るたびに、バックは未知への恐怖に襲われた

he was glad each time another dog was taken, rather than himself.
彼は、自分ではなく他の犬が連れて行かれるたびに嬉しかった

But finally, Buck's turn came with the arrival of a strange man.
しかし、ついに、奇妙な男の出現により、バックの番が来た

He was small, wiry, and spoke in broken English and curses.
彼は小柄で、筋肉質で、片言の英語と汚い言葉で話した

"Sacredam!" he yelled when he laid eyes on Buck's frame.
「神聖だ！」彼はバックの体格を見て叫んだ

"That's one damn bully dog! Eh? How much?" he asked aloud.
「あれは本当にいじめっ子だ！え？いくらだ？」と彼は大声で尋ねた

"Three hundred, and he's a present at that price,"
「300ドルで彼はプレゼントだ」

"Since it's government money, you shouldn't complain, Perrault."
「政府のお金なんだから文句を言うべきじゃないよ、ペロー」

Perrault grinned at the deal he had just made with the man.
ペローはその男と交わしたばかりの取引にニヤリと笑った

The price of dogs had soared due to the sudden demand.
突然の需要により犬の値段が高騰した

Three hundred dollars wasn't unfair for such a fine beast.
こんなに素晴らしい獣に対して、300ドルは不当ではない

The Canadian Government would not lose anything in the deal
カナダ政府はこの取引で何も失うことはない

Nor would their official dispatches be delayed in transit.
また、公式の派遣が輸送中に遅れることもありません

Perrault knew dogs well, and could see Buck was something rare.
ペローは犬をよく知っていたので、バックが珍しい犬だと分かっていた

"One in ten ten-thousand," he thought, as he studied Buck's build.
「一万分の一だ」と彼はバックの体格を研究しながら思った

Buck saw the money change hands, but showed no surprise.
バックはお金が手渡されるのを見たが、驚いた様子はなかった

Soon he and Curly, a gentle Newfoundland, were led away.

すぐに彼と温厚なニューファンドランド犬の縮れたは連れて行かれました

They followed the little man from the red sweater's yard.

彼らは赤いセーターを着た人の庭からその小男の後を追った

That was the last Buck ever saw of the man with the wooden club.

それがバックが木の棍棒を持った男を見た最後の時だった

From the Narwhal's deck he watched Seattle fade into the distance.

彼はイッカク号のデッキからシアトルが遠くに消えていくのを眺めた

It was also the last time he ever saw the warm Southland.

それは彼が暖かい南国を見た最後の機会でもありました

Perrault took them below deck, and left them with François.

ペローは彼らを船底に連れて行き、フランソワに預けた

François was a black-faced giant with rough, calloused hands.

フランソワは、顔が黒く、手が荒れてタコだらけの巨漢だった

He was dark and swarthy; a half-breed French-Canadian.

彼は肌が浅黒く、フランス系カナダ人の混血だった

To Buck, these men were of a kind he had never seen before.

バックにとって、これらの男たちは今まで見たことのない種類の男たちだった

He would come to know many such men in the days ahead.

彼はその後、そのような男性を数多く知ることになるだろう

He did not grow fond of them, but he came to respect them.

彼は彼らを好きになったわけではないが、尊敬するようになった

They were fair and wise, and not easily fooled by any dog.

彼らは公平で賢く、どんな犬にも簡単に騙されることはありませんでした

They judged dogs calmly, and punished only when deserved.
彼らは犬を冷静に判断し、罰に値する場合にのみ罰を与えた

In the Narwhal's lower deck, Buck and Curly met two dogs.
イッカク号の下甲板で、バックと縮れたは二匹の犬に出会った

One was a large white dog from far-off, icy Spitzbergen.
一匹は遠く離れた氷に覆われたスピッツベルゲン島から来た大きな白い犬でした

He'd once sailed with a whaler and joined a survey group.
彼はかつて捕鯨船に乗って調査団に加わったことがある

He was friendly in a sly, underhanded and crafty fashion.
彼はずる賢く、陰険で、ずる賢いやり方で友好的だった

At their first meal, he stole a piece of meat from Buck's pan.
最初の食事のとき、彼はバックのフライパンから肉を一切れ盗みました

Buck jumped to punish him, but François's whip struck first.
バックは彼を罰するために飛びかかったが、フランソワの鞭が先に当たった

The white thief yelped, and Buck reclaimed the stolen bone.
白人の泥棒は悲鳴をあげ、バックは盗まれた骨を取り戻した

That fairness impressed Buck, and François earned his respect.
その公平さはバックに感銘を与え、フランソワは彼の尊敬を得た

The other dog gave no greeting, and wanted none in return.
もう一匹の犬は挨拶もせず、挨拶の返事も求めませんでした

He didn't steal food, nor sniff at the new arrivals with interest.
彼は食べ物を盗んだり、新しく来たものを興味深く嗅いだりしませんでした

This dog was grim and quiet, gloomy and slow-moving.

この犬は陰気で静かで、陰気で動きが遅かった

He warned Curly to stay away by simply glaring at her.
彼はただ睨みつけるだけで縮れたに近寄らないように警告した

His message was clear; leave me alone or there'll be trouble.
彼のメッセージは明確でした私を放っておいてくれ、さもないと問題が起きるぞ、というものでした

He was called Dave, and he barely noticed his surroundings.
彼はデイブと呼ばれ、周囲の状況をほとんど気にしていませんでした

He slept often, ate quietly, and yawned now and again.
彼はよく眠り、静かに食事をし、時々あくびをしていた

The ship hummed constantly with the beating propeller below.
船は下でプロペラが鼓動する音とともに絶えずブンブンと音を立てていた

Days passed with little change, but the weather got colder.
あまり変化のない日々が過ぎていきましたが、天気は寒くなってきました

Buck could feel it in his bones, and noticed the others did too.
バックはそれを骨の髄まで感じ、他の人たちもそう感じていることに気づいた

Then one morning, the propeller stopped and all was still.
そしてある朝、プロペラが止まり、すべてが静かになりました

An energy swept through the ship; something had changed.
エネルギーが船中に広がり、何かが変わった

François came down, clipped them on leashes, and brought them up.
フランソワは降りてきて、犬たちにリードをつけ、連れて帰りました

Buck stepped out and found the ground soft, white, and cold.

バックは外に出て、地面が柔らかく、白く、冷たいことに気づいた

He jumped back in alarm and snorted in total confusion.
彼は驚いて飛び退き、完全に混乱した様子で鼻を鳴らした

Strange white stuff was falling from the gray sky.
灰色の空から奇妙な白いものが落ちてきました

He shook himself, but the white flakes kept landing on him.
彼は体を震わせたが、白い雪片は彼の上に降り注ぎ続けた

He sniffed the white stuff carefully and licked at a few icy bits.
彼はその白いものを注意深く嗅ぎ、氷のようなものをいくつか舐めた

The powder burned like fire, then vanished right off his tongue.
粉は火のように燃え、舌の上から消えていった

Buck tried again, puzzled by the odd vanishing coldness.
バックは、奇妙に消えていく冷たさに困惑しながら、もう一度試してみた

The men around him laughed, and Buck felt embarrassed.
周りの男たちは笑い、バックは恥ずかしくなった

He didn't know why, but he was ashamed of his reaction.
彼は理由は知らなかったが、自分の反応を恥じた

It was his first experience with snow, and it confused him.
それは彼にとって初めての雪の経験であり、彼は混乱した

The Law of Club and Fang
棍棒と牙の法則

Buck's first day on the Dyea beach felt like a terrible nightmare.

バックにとってダイアビーチでの初日はひどい悪夢のようだった

Each hour brought new shocks and unexpected changes for Buck.

毎時間ごとに、バックは新たな衝撃と予期せぬ変化に見舞われた

He had been pulled from civilization and thrown into wild chaos.

彼は文明から引き離され、激しい混乱の中に放り込まれた

This was no sunny, lazy life with boredom and rest.

これは退屈と休息を伴う、陽気で怠惰な生活ではありませんでした

There was no peace, no rest, and no moment without danger.

平和も休息もなく、危険のない瞬間もなかった

Confusion ruled everything, and danger was always close.

混乱がすべてを支配し、危険は常に身近に迫っていました

Buck had to stay alert because these men and dogs were different.

バックは、これらの男たちと犬たちが異なっていたので、警戒を怠ってはならなかった

They were not from towns; they were wild and without mercy.

彼らは町から来たわけではなく、野蛮で慈悲のない者たちでした

These men and dogs only knew the law of club and fang.

これらの男と犬は棍棒と牙の法則しか知らなかった

Buck had never seen dogs fight like these savage huskies.

バックは、これらの獰猛なハスキー犬のように戦う犬を見たことがなかった

His first experience taught him a lesson he would never forget.

その最初の経験は彼に決して忘れることのない教訓を与えた

He was lucky it was not him, or he would have died too.

それが彼でなかったのは幸運だった、そうでなければ彼も死んでいただろう

Curly was the one who suffered while Buck watched and learned.

バックが見守りながら学んでいる間、苦しんだのは縮れただった

They had made camp near a store built from logs.

彼らは丸太で建てられた店の近くにキャンプを張っていた

Curly tried to be friendly to a large, wolf-like husky.

縮れたは、狼のような大きなハスキー犬に優しくしようとしました

The husky was smaller than Curly, but looked wild and mean.

ハスキーは縮れたより小さかったが、野性的で凶暴な様子だった

Without warning, he jumped and slashed her face open.

彼は何の前触れもなく飛び上がり、彼女の顔を切り裂いた

His teeth cut from her eye down to her jaw in one move.

彼の歯は彼女の目から顎まで一気に切り裂いた

This was how wolves fought—hit fast and jump away.

これがオオカミの戦い方です素早く攻撃して、飛び去るのです

But there was more to learn than from that one attack.

しかし、その攻撃から学ぶべきことはもっとたくさんありました

Dozens of huskies rushed in and made a silent circle.

数十匹のハスキー犬が駆け寄ってきて、静かに輪を作った

They watched closely and licked their lips with hunger.

彼らはじっと見つめ、空腹で唇をなめました

Buck didn't understand their silence or their eager eyes.

バックは彼らの沈黙や熱心な視線の意味を理解していなかった

Curly rushed to attack the husky a second time.

縮れたは再びハスキー犬を攻撃しようと突進した

He used his chest to knock her over with a strong move.

彼は胸を使って強い動きで彼女を倒した

She fell on her side and could not get back up.

彼女は横に倒れてしまい、起き上がることができませんでした

That was what the others had been waiting for all along.

それは他の人たちもずっと待っていたものだった

The huskies jumped on her, yelping and snarling in a frenzy.

ハスキー犬たちは狂ったように吠えながら彼女に飛びかかった

She screamed as they buried her under a pile of dogs.

彼女は犬の山の下に埋められたとき、叫び声をあげた

The attack was so fast that Buck froze in place with shock.

攻撃があまりにも速かったので、バックはショックでその場に凍りついた

He saw Spitz stick out his tongue in a way that looked like a laugh.

彼はスピッツが笑っているように見える形で舌を突き出しているのを見た

François grabbed an axe and ran straight into the group of dogs.

フランソワは斧を掴み、まっすぐ犬の群れの中に突進した

Three other men used clubs to help beat the huskies away.

他の3人の男は棍棒を使ってハスキー犬を追い払った

In just two minutes, the fight was over and the dogs were gone.

わずか2分で戦いは終わり、犬たちはいなくなっていました

Curly lay dead in the red, trampled snow, her body torn apart.
縮れたは、体を引き裂かれ、踏みつけられた赤い雪の上に死んで横たわっていた

A dark-skinned man stood over her, cursing the brutal scene.
黒い肌の男が彼女の前に立ち、残酷な光景を罵った

The memory stayed with Buck and haunted his dreams at night.
その記憶はバックの心の中に残り、毎晩夢に現れた

That was the way here; no fairness, no second chance.
ここではそれが普通だった公平さもなければ二度目のチャンスもない

Once a dog fell, the others would kill without mercy.
一匹の犬が倒れると、他の犬は容赦なく殺します

Buck decided then that he would never allow himself to fall.
バックはそのとき、自分は決して落ちないと決心した

Spitz stuck out his tongue again and laughed at the blood.
スピッツはまた舌を出して血を見て笑った

From that moment on, Buck hated Spitz with all his heart.
その瞬間から、バックは心底スピッツを憎むようになった

Before Buck could recover from Curly's death, something new happened.
バックが縮れたの死から立ち直る前に、新たな出来事が起こった

François came over and strapped something around Buck's body.
フランソワがやって来て、バックの体に何かを巻き付けました

It was a harness like the ones used on horses at the ranch.
それは牧場で馬に使われるような馬具でした

As Buck had seen horses work, now he was made to work too.

バックは馬が働くのを見てきたので、今度は自分も働かされることになった

He had to pull François on a sled into the forest nearby.
彼はフランソワをそりに乗せて近くの森まで引っ張って行かなければなりませんでした

Then he had to pull back a load of heavy firewood.
それから、彼は重い薪を積んで引き戻さなければなりませんでした

Buck was proud, so it hurt him to be treated like a work animal.
バックはプライドの高い人だったので、労働動物のように扱われるのは辛かった

But he was wise and didn't try to fight the new situation.
しかし彼は賢明だったので、新たな状況に逆らおうとはしなかった

He accepted his new life and gave his best in every task.
彼は新しい人生を受け入れ、あらゆる仕事に最善を尽くしました

Everything about the work was strange and unfamiliar to him.
彼にとって、その仕事に関するすべてが奇妙で未知のものだった

François was strict and demanded obedience without delay.
フランソワは厳格で、遅滞なく従うことを要求した

His whip made sure that every command was followed at once.
彼の鞭はすべての命令がすぐに従うことを確実にした

Dave was the wheeler, the dog nearest the sled behind Buck.
デイブは車輪の引き手で、バックの後ろでそりに一番近い犬でした

Dave bit Buck on the back legs if he made a mistake.
デイブは、バックがミスをすると後ろ足を噛みました

Spitz was the lead dog, skilled and experienced in the role.
スピッツはリーダー犬であり、その役割に熟練しており、経験豊富でした

Spitz could not reach Buck easily, but still corrected him.

スピッツはバックに簡単には辿り着けなかったが、それでも彼を訂正した

He growled harshly or pulled the sled in ways that taught Buck.

彼は荒々しく唸ったり、バックに教えるようなやり方でそりを引いたりした

Under this training, Buck learned faster than any of them expected.

この訓練により、バックは誰もが予想していたよりも早く学習しました

He worked hard and learned from both François and the other dogs.

彼は一生懸命働き、フランソワと他の犬たちから学びました

By the time they returned, Buck already knew the key commands.

彼らが戻ったとき、バックはすでに重要なコマンドを覚えていました

He learned to stop at the sound of "ho" from François.

彼はフランソワから「ホ」という音で止まることを教わりました

He learned when he had to pull the sled and run.

彼はそりを引いて走らなければならない時を学びました

He learned to turn wide at bends in the trail without trouble.

彼は道の曲がり角で問題なく大きく曲がることを学んだ

He also learned to avoid Dave when the sled went downhill fast.

彼はまた、そりが急に坂を下りてきたときにデイブを避けることも学びました

"They're very good dogs," François proudly told Perrault.

「彼らはとても良い犬だ」フランソワは誇らしげにペローに言った

"That Buck pulls like hell—I teach him quick as anything."

「あの雄鹿はものすごく引っ張るから、とにかく速く引っ張るように教えてやったんだ」

Later that day, Perrault came back with two more husky dogs.
その日遅く、ペローはさらに2匹のハスキー犬を連れて戻ってきた

Their names were Billee and Joe, and they were brothers.
彼らの名前はビリーとジョーで、兄弟でした

They came from the same mother, but were not alike at all.
彼らは同じ母親から生まれましたが、まったく似ていませんでした

Billee was sweet-natured and too friendly with everyone.
ビリーは優しい性格で、誰に対してもとてもフレンドリーでした

Joe was the opposite—quiet, angry, and always snarling.
ジョーは正反対で、静かで、怒っていて、いつも怒鳴っていました

Buck greeted them in a friendly way and was calm with both.
バックは二人に友好的に挨拶し、二人に対して穏やかに接した

Dave paid no attention to them and stayed silent as usual.
デイブは彼らに注意を払わず、いつものように黙っていた

Spitz attacked first Billee, then Joe, to show his dominance.
スピッツは自分の優位性を示すために、まずビリーを攻撃し、次にジョーを攻撃した

Billee wagged his tail and tried to be friendly to Spitz.
ビリーは尻尾を振ってスピッツに優しくしようとしました

When that didn't work, he tried to run away instead.
それがうまくいかなかったとき、彼は代わりに逃げようとしました

He cried sadly when Spitz bit him hard on the side.
スピッツが彼の脇腹を強く噛んだとき、彼は悲しそうに泣きました

But Joe was very different and refused to be bullied.

しかし、ジョーは他の子とは全く違っていて、いじめられることを拒否しました

Every time Spitz came near, Joe spun to face him fast.

スピッツが近づくたびに、ジョーは素早く回転してスピッツのほうを向いた

His fur bristled, his lips curled, and his teeth snapped wildly.

彼の毛は逆立ち、唇は歪んで、歯は激しくカチカチと音を立てた

Joe's eyes gleamed with fear and rage, daring Spitz to strike.

ジョーの目は恐怖と怒りで輝き、スピッツに攻撃を挑発した

Spitz gave up the fight and turned away, humiliated and angry.

スピッツは屈辱と怒りを感じながら戦いを諦め、立ち去った

He took out his frustration on poor Billee and chased him away.

彼はかわいそうなビリーに不満をぶつけ、彼を追い払った

That evening, Perrault added one more dog to the team.

その夜、ペローはチームにもう一匹の犬を加えました

This dog was old, lean, and covered in battle scars.

この犬は年老いて、痩せていて、戦いの傷跡で覆われていました

One of his eyes was missing, but the other flashed with power.

彼の目は片方は欠けていたが、もう片方は力強く輝いていた

The new dog's name was Solleks, which meant the Angry One.

新しい犬の名前はソレックス、つまり「怒った犬」という意味でした

Like Dave, Solleks asked nothing from others, and gave nothing back.

デイブと同様に、ソレックスは他人に何も求めず、何も返さなかった

When Solleks walked slowly into camp, even Spitz stayed away.

ソレックスがゆっくりとキャンプに歩いて入っていくと、スピッツさえも近寄らなかった

He had a strange habit that Buck was unlucky to discover.

彼には奇妙な習慣があったが、バックはそれを不運にも発見してしまった

Solleks hated being approached on the side where he was blind.

ソレックスさんは、自分の目が見えていない側から近づかれるのが大嫌いだった

Buck did not know this and made that mistake by accident.

バックはこれを知らず、偶然にその間違いを犯しました

Solleks spun around and slashed Buck's shoulder deep and fast.

ソレックスはくるりと回転し、バックの肩を深く素早く切りつけた

From that moment on, Buck never came near Solleks' blind side.

その瞬間から、バックはソレックスの死角に近づくことはなかった

They never had trouble again for the rest of their time together.

彼らが一緒に過ごした残りの期間、再び問題が起こることはなかった

Solleks wanted only to be left alone, like quiet Dave.

ソレックスは、静かなデイブのように、ただ一人になることを望んでいた

But Buck would later learn they each had another secret goal.

しかし、バックは後に、彼らがそれぞれ別の秘密の目的を持っていたことを知ることになる

That night Buck faced a new and troubling challenge—how to sleep.

その夜、バックは新たな困難な課題、つまりどうやって眠るかという問題に直面した

The tent glowed warmly with candlelight in the snowy field.
雪原の中のテントはろうそくの明かりで暖かく輝いていた

Buck walked inside, thinking he could rest there like before.
バックは、以前のようにそこで休めるだろうと思って中に入った

But Perrault and François yelled at him and threw pans.
しかしペローとフランソワは彼に怒鳴りつけ、鍋を投げつけた

Shocked and confused, Buck ran out into the freezing cold.
ショックを受けて混乱したバックは、凍えるような寒さの中へ飛び出しました

A bitter wind stung his wounded shoulder and froze his paws.
ひどい風が彼の傷ついた肩を刺し、彼の足を凍らせた

He lay down in the snow and tried to sleep out in the open.
彼は雪の上に横たわり、戸外で眠ろうとした

But the cold soon forced him to get back up, shaking badly.
しかし、寒さのせいで、彼はすぐにひどく震えながら起き上がらざるを得ませんでした

He wandered through the camp, trying to find a warmer spot.
彼は暖かい場所を探してキャンプ場を歩き回った

But every corner was just as cold as the one before.
しかし、どの角も前と同じように寒かった

Sometimes savage dogs jumped at him from the darkness.
時々、暗闇の中から凶暴な犬が彼に飛びかかってくることもありました

Buck bristled his fur, bared his teeth, and snarled with warning.
バックは毛を逆立て、歯をむき出しにして、警告するように唸った

He was learning fast, and the other dogs backed off quickly.
彼は学習が早く、他の犬たちはすぐに後退しました

Still, he had no place to sleep, and no idea what to do.

それでも、彼には寝る場所もなく、何をすればいいのかもわからなかった

At last, a thought came to him — check on his team-mates.

ついに、彼はチームメイトの様子を確認するという考えを思いつきました

He returned to their area and was surprised to find them gone.

彼は彼らの地域に戻り、彼らがいなくなっていることに驚きました

Again he searched the camp, but still could not find them.

彼は再びキャンプ内を捜索したが、やはり彼らを見つけることはできなかった

He knew they could not be in the tent, or he would be too.

彼らがテントの中にいるはずがない、そうでなければ自分もテントの中にいることになる、と彼は知っていた

So where had all the dogs gone in this frozen camp?

それで、この凍ったキャンプで犬たちはどこへ行ってしまったのでしょうか?

Buck, cold and miserable, slowly circled around the tent.

寒さと惨めさを感じたバックはゆっくりとテントの周りを回った

Suddenly, his front legs sank into soft snow and startled him.

突然、前足が柔らかい雪の中に沈み、彼は驚きました

Something wriggled under his feet, and he jumped back in fear.

足元で何かがうごめいたため、彼は恐怖で後ずさりした

He growled and snarled, not knowing what lay beneath the snow.

彼は雪の下に何があるのかも知らずに、うなり声をあげた

Then he heard a friendly little bark that eased his fear.

すると、友好的な小さな吠え声が聞こえてきて、彼の恐怖は和らぎました

He sniffed the air and came closer to see what was hidden.

彼は空気を嗅いで、何が隠されているかを見るために近づいてきました

Under the snow, curled into a warm ball, was little Billee.
雪の下で、暖かいボールのように丸まっているのは、小さなビリーでした

Billee wagged his tail and licked Buck's face to greet him.
ビリーは尻尾を振ってバックの顔を舐めて挨拶しました

Buck saw how Billee had made a sleeping place in the snow.
バックはビリーが雪の中に寝場所を作っているのを見た

He had dug down and used his own heat to stay warm.
彼は地面を掘り、自分の体温を利用して暖をとっていた

Buck had learned another lesson—this was how the dogs slept.
バックはまた別の教訓を学んだ犬たちはこうやって眠るのだ

He picked a spot and started digging his own hole in the snow.
彼は場所を選び、雪の中に自分の穴を掘り始めました

At first, he moved around too much and wasted energy.
最初は動き回りすぎてエネルギーを無駄にしていました

But soon his body warmed the space, and he felt safe.
しかし、すぐに彼の体はその空間を温め、彼は安心した

He curled up tightly, and before long he was fast asleep.
彼は体をしっかりと丸めて、すぐにぐっすりと眠ってしまいました

The day had been long and hard, and Buck was exhausted.
その日は長くてつらい一日だったので、バックは疲れ果てていた

He slept deeply and comfortably, though his dreams were wild.
彼は荒々しい夢を見ていたにもかかわらず、深く心地よく眠った

He growled and barked in his sleep, twisting as he dreamed.
彼は夢を見ながら体をよじりながら、寝言を言ったり吠えたりした

Buck didn't wake up until the camp was already coming to life.
バックはキャンプが活気づき始めるまで目を覚まさなかった

At first, he didn't know where he was or what had happened.
最初、彼は自分がどこにいるのか、何が起こったのか分かりませんでした

Snow had fallen overnight and completely buried his body.
一晩中に雪が降り、彼の遺体が完全に埋もれてしまった

The snow pressed in around him, tight on all sides.
雪は彼の周囲にぎっしりと押し付けられていた

Suddenly a wave of fear rushed through Buck's entire body.
突然、恐怖の波がバックの全身を駆け巡った

It was the fear of being trapped, a fear from deep instincts.
それは閉じ込められることへの恐怖であり、深い本能からくる恐怖でした

Though he had never seen a trap, the fear lived inside him.
彼は罠を見たことがなかったが、心の中では恐怖が残っていた

He was a tame dog, but now his old wild instincts were waking.
彼は飼いならされた犬だったが、今では昔の野生の本能が目覚めていた

Buck's muscles tensed, and his fur stood up all over his back.
バックの筋肉は緊張し、背中の毛が逆立った

He snarled fiercely and sprang straight up through the snow.
彼は激しく唸り声をあげ、雪の中をまっすぐに飛び上がった

Snow flew in every direction as he burst into the daylight.
彼が日光の中に飛び出すと、雪が四方八方に舞い上がった

Even before landing, Buck saw the camp spread out before him.

着陸する前から、バックは目の前に広がるキャンプを見た

He remembered everything from the day before, all at once.
彼は前日の出来事をすべて一気に思い出した

He remembered strolling with Manuel and ending up in this place.
彼はマヌエルと一緒に散歩してこの場所にたどり着いたことを思い出した

He remembered digging the hole and falling asleep in the cold.
彼は穴を掘って寒さの中で眠りに落ちたことを思い出した

Now he was awake, and the wild world around him was clear.
今、彼は目を覚まし、周囲の荒々しい世界がはっきりと見えていた

A shout from François hailed Buck's sudden appearance.
フランソワはバックの突然の出現を歓迎する叫び声をあげた

"What did I say?" the dog-driver cried loudly to Perrault.
「私が何て言ったの？」犬の御者はペローに向かって大声で叫んだ

"That Buck for sure learns quick as anything," François added.
「あの雄鹿は間違いなく、ものすごく早く学習するね」とフランソワは付け加えた

Perrault nodded gravely, clearly pleased with the result.
ペローは結果に明らかに満足し、重々しくうなずいた

As a courier for the Canadian Government, he carried dispatches.
彼はカナダ政府の伝令として、伝言を運んだ

He was eager to find the best dogs for his important mission.
彼は重要な任務に最適な犬を見つけることに熱心だった

He felt especially pleased now that Buck was part of the team.

彼はバックがチームの一員になったことを特に嬉しく思った

Three more huskies were added to the team within an hour.
1 時間以内にさらに 3
匹のハスキー犬がチームに加わりました

That brought the total number of dogs on the team to nine.
これにより、チームの犬の数は合計 9 匹になりました

Within fifteen minutes all the dogs were in their harnesses.
15分以内に、すべての犬がハーネスを着けました

The sled team was swinging up the trail toward Dyea Cañon.
そりチームはダイア渓谷に向かって道を登っていた

Buck felt glad to be leaving, even if the work ahead was hard.
バックは、たとえ今後の仕事が大変であっても、去ることができて嬉しかった

He found he did not particularly despise the labor or the cold.
彼は労働や寒さを特に嫌っているわけではないことに気づいた

He was surprised by the eagerness that filled the whole team.
彼はチーム全体に満ち溢れた熱意に驚いた

Even more surprising was the change that had come over Dave and Solleks.
さらに驚いたのは、デイブとソレックスに起こった変化だった

These two dogs were entirely different when they were harnessed.
この二匹の犬は、ハーネスをつけたときはまったく違っていました

Their passiveness and lack of concern had completely disappeared.
彼らの消極的な態度や無関心は完全に消え去っていました

They were alert and active, and eager to do their work well.

彼らは機敏で活動的であり、仕事をうまくやり遂げることに熱心でした

They grew fiercely irritated at anything that caused delay or confusion.
彼らは、遅延や混乱を引き起こすものに対して激しくイライラするようになった

The hard work on the reins was the center of their entire being.
手綱を握る懸命な仕事が彼らの全存在の中心でした

Sled pulling seemed to be the only thing they truly enjoyed.
そりを引くことが彼らが本当に楽しんでいる唯一のことのようでした

Dave was at the back of the group, closest to the sled itself.
デイブはグループの最後尾、そりに一番近かった

Buck was placed in front of Dave, and Solleks pulled ahead of Buck.
バックはデイブの前に配置され、ソレックスはバックの前に進みました

The rest of the dogs were strung out ahead in a single file.
残りの犬たちは一列になって前に並んでいた

The lead position at the front was filled by Spitz.
先頭の座はスピッツが占めた

Buck had been placed between Dave and Solleks for instruction.
バックは指導のためにデイブとソレックスの間に置かれていた

He was a quick learner, and they were firm and capable teachers.
彼は学習が早く、教師たちは厳格で有能でした

They never allowed Buck to remain in error for long.
彼らはバックが長期間にわたって誤ったままでいることを決して許さなかった

They taught their lessons with sharp teeth when needed.
彼らは必要に応じて鋭い歯で教訓を教えました

Dave was fair and showed a quiet, serious kind of wisdom.
デイブは公平で、静かで真剣な知恵を示しました

He never bit Buck without a good reason to do so.
彼は、正当な理由がない限り、決してバックを噛むことはなかった

But he never failed to bite when Buck needed correction.
しかし、バックが矯正を必要としているときは、彼は決して噛み付かなかった

François's whip was always ready and backed up their authority.
フランソワの鞭は常に準備されており、彼らの権威を支えていた

Buck soon found it was better to obey than to fight back.
バックはすぐに、反撃するよりも従うほうがよいことに気づいた

Once, during a short rest, Buck got tangled in the reins.
一度、短い休憩中に、バックは手綱に絡まってしまいました

He delayed the start and confused the team's movement.
彼はスタートを遅らせ、チームの動きを混乱させた

Dave and Solleks flew at him and gave him a rough beating.
デイブとソレックスは彼に飛びかかり、激しく殴りつけた

The tangle only got worse, but Buck learned his lesson well.
もつれは悪化するばかりだったが、バックは教訓をよく学んだ

From then on, he kept the reins taut, and worked carefully.
それ以来、彼は手綱をしっかりと締め、慎重に作業を続けた

Before the day ended, Buck had mastered much of his task.
その日が終わる前に、バックは自分の任務の大半をマスターした

His teammates almost stopped correcting or biting him.
チームメイトは彼を叱ったり噛んだりすることをほとんどやめました

François's whip cracked through the air less and less often.
フランソワの鞭が空気を切る音はだんだん小さくなっていった

Perrault even lifted Buck's feet and carefully examined each paw.

ペローはバックの足を持ち上げて、それぞれの足を注意深く調べました

It had been a hard day's run, long and exhausting for them all.

彼ら全員にとって、それは長くて疲れる、厳しい一日のランニングだった

They travelled up the Cañon, through Sheep Camp, and past the Scales.

彼らはキャニオンを登り、シープキャンプを通り、スケールズを過ぎました

They crossed the timber line, then glaciers and snowdrifts many feet deep.

彼らは森林限界を越え、さらに何フィートも深い氷河と雪の吹きだまりを越えた

They climbed the great cold and forbidding Chilkoot Divide.

彼らは、とても寒くて恐ろしいチルクート分水嶺を登りました

That high ridge stood between salt water and the frozen interior.

その高い尾根は塩水と凍った内陸部の間に位置していた

The mountains guarded the sad and lonely North with ice and steep climbs.

山々は氷と険しい坂道で、悲しく孤独な北を守っていた

They made good time down a long chain of lakes below the divide.

彼らは分水嶺の下の長い湖群を順調に下っていった

Those lakes filled the ancient craters of extinct volcanoes.

これらの湖は死火山の古代の火口を埋め尽くしたものでした

Late that night, they reached a large camp at Lake Bennett.

その夜遅く、彼らはベネット湖の大きなキャンプ地に到着した

Thousands of gold seekers were there, building boats for spring.

何千人もの金採掘者がそこに集まり、春に向けて船を建造していた

The ice was going break up soon, and they had to be ready.

氷はすぐに解けそうだったので、彼らは準備をする必要がありました

Buck dug his hole in the snow and fell into a deep sleep.

バックは雪の中に穴を掘り、深い眠りに落ちた

He slept like a working man, exhausted from the harsh day of toil.

彼は、厳しい一日の労働で疲れ果てた労働者のように眠った

But too early in the darkness, he was dragged from sleep.

しかし、暗闇の中で、彼は眠りから引きずり起こされた

He was harnessed with his mates again and attached to the sled.

彼は再び仲間たちと馬具を着けられ、そりに繋がれた

That day they made forty miles, because the snow was well trodden.

その日、雪はよく踏み固められていたので、彼らは40マイル進んだ

The next day, and for many days after, the snow was soft.

翌日、そしてその後何日も、雪は柔らかくなっていました

They had to make the path themselves, working harder and moving slower.

彼らは自分たちで道を切り開かなければならず、より懸命に働き、よりゆっくりと進みました

Usually, Perrault walked ahead of the team with webbed snowshoes.

通常、ペローは水かきのあるスノーシューを履いてチームの先頭を歩いていた

His steps packed the snow, making it easier for the sled to move.

彼の足取りで雪が踏み固められ、そりが動きやすくなった

François, who steered from the gee-pole, sometimes took over.

ジーポールから舵を取っていたフランソワが時々操縦を引き継いだ

But it was rare that François took the lead

しかしフランソワがリードするのは稀だった

because Perrault was in a rush to deliver the letters and parcels.

ペローは手紙や小包を配達するのに急いでいたからです

Perrault was proud of his knowledge of snow, and especially ice.

ペローは雪、特に氷に関する知識に誇りを持っていました

That knowledge was essential, because fall ice was dangerously thin.

秋の氷は危険なほど薄かったため、その知識は不可欠でした

Where water flowed fast beneath the surface, there was no ice at all.

地表の下で水が速く流れる場所には、氷はまったくありませんでした

Day after day, the same routine repeated without end.

来る日も来る日も、同じ繰り返しが終わりなく続いた

Buck toiled endlessly in the reins from dawn until night.

バックは夜明けから夜まで手綱を握りしめ、休みなく働き続けた

They left camp in the dark, long before the sun had risen.

彼らは太陽が昇るずっと前に、暗闇の中キャンプを出発した

By the time daylight came, many miles were already behind them.

夜が明ける頃には、彼らはすでに何マイルも離れたところまで来ていた

They pitched camp after dark, eating fish and burrowing into snow.

彼らは暗くなってからキャンプを張り、魚を食べたり雪の中に穴を掘ったりした

Buck was always hungry and never truly satisfied with his ration.

バックはいつも空腹で、配給された食料に決して満足することはありませんでした

He received a pound and a half of dried salmon each day.

彼は毎日1ポンド半の干し鮭を受け取った

But the food seemed to vanish inside him, leaving hunger behind.

しかし、食べ物は彼の体内から消え去り、空腹だけが残ったようだった

He suffered from constant pangs of hunger, and dreamed of more food.

彼は絶え間ない空腹感に苦しみ、もっと食べ物が欲しいと夢見ていた

The other dogs got only one pound of food, but they stayed strong.

他の犬たちはたった1ポンドの食べ物しか与えられなかったが、それでも元気に生き延びた

They were smaller, and had been born into the northern life.

彼らは小柄で、北の暮らしの中で生まれてきた

He swiftly lost the fastidiousness which had marked his old life.

彼は昔の生活を特徴づけていた几帳面さをすぐに失った

He had been a dainty eater, but now that was no longer possible.

彼は以前は美味しいものを食べる人だったが、今はもうそれができなくなっていた

His mates finished first and robbed him of his unfinished ration.

仲間が先に食べ終えて、残っていた食料を奪い取った

Once they began there was no way to defend his food from them.

一度彼らが攻撃を始めると、彼らから食べ物を守る方法はなくなりました

While he fought off two or three dogs, the others stole the rest.

彼が二、三匹の犬と戦っている間に、他の犬たちが残りの犬を盗んでいった

To fix this, he began eating as fast as the others ate.

これを直すために、彼は他の人と同じ速さで食べ始めました

Hunger pushed him so hard that he even took food not his own.

空腹に押しつぶされそうになった彼は、自分のものではない食べ物さえも口にした

He watched the others and learned quickly from their actions.

彼は他の人達を観察し、彼らの行動からすぐに学びました

He saw Pike, a new dog, steal a slice of bacon from Perrault.

彼は、新しい犬のパイクがペローからベーコンのスライスを盗むのを目撃しました

Pike had waited until Perrault's back was turned to steal the bacon.

パイクはペローが背を向けるまで待ってベーコンを盗んだ

The next day, Buck copied Pike and stole the whole chunk.

翌日、バックはパイクの真似をして、その塊を全部盗みました

A great uproar followed, but Buck was not suspected.

大きな騒動が起こったが、バックは疑われなかった

Dub, a clumsy dog who always got caught, was punished instead.

いつも捕まってしまう不器用な犬のダブが代わりに罰せられました

That first theft marked Buck as a dog fit to survive the North.

その最初の窃盗により、バックは北部で生き残れる犬として名声を得た

He showed he could adapt to new conditions and learn quickly.

彼は新しい状況に適応し、素早く学習できることを示した

Without such adaptability, he would have died swiftly and badly.

そのような適応力がなければ、彼はすぐにひどい死を遂げていたでしょう

It also marked the breakdown of his moral nature and past values.

それはまた、彼の道徳心と過去の価値観の崩壊を意味した

In the Southland, he had lived under the law of love and kindness.

サウスランドでは、彼は愛と優しさの法則の下で暮らしていた

There it made sense to respect property and other dogs' feelings.

そこでは、財産や他の犬の感情を尊重することが理にかなっています

But the Northland followed the law of club and the law of fang.

しかし、ノースランドは棍棒の法則と牙の法則に従っていた

Whoever respected old values here was foolish and would fail.

ここで古い価値観を尊重する者は愚かであり、失敗するだろう

Buck did not reason all this out in his mind.

バックはこれらすべてを頭の中で推論したわけではなかった

He was fit, and so he adjusted without needing to think.

彼は健康だったので、考える必要もなく適応しました

All his life, he had never run away from a fight.

彼は生涯を通じて一度も戦いから逃げたことがなかった

But the wooden club of the man in the red sweater changed that rule.

しかし、赤いセーターを着た男の棍棒がそのルールを変えた

Now he followed a deeper, older code written into his being.

今、彼は自分の中に刻み込まれた、より深く、より古い規範に従っていた

He did not steal out of pleasure, but from the pain of hunger.

彼は快楽のために盗んだのではなく、飢えの苦しみから盗んだのです

He never robbed openly, but stole with cunning and care.

彼は決して公然と盗みを働いたことはなく、狡猾かつ慎重に盗みを働いた

He acted out of respect for the wooden club and fear of the fang.

彼は木の棍棒への敬意と牙への恐怖から行動した

In short, he did what was easier and safer than not doing it.

つまり、彼は何もしないより簡単で安全なことをしたのです

His development—or perhaps his return to old instincts—was fast.

彼の成長、あるいは昔の本能への回帰は速かった

His muscles hardened until they felt as strong as iron.

彼の筋肉は鉄のように硬くなったように感じた

He no longer cared about pain, unless it was serious.

彼は、深刻な場合を除いて、痛みを気にしなくなった

He became efficient inside and out, wasting nothing at all.

彼は、まったく無駄をすることなく、内外ともに効率的になりました

He could eat things that were vile, rotten, or hard to digest.

彼は、不味いもの、腐ったもの、消化しにくいものを食べることができました

Whatever he ate, his stomach used every last bit of value.

何を食べても、胃がその価値をすべて使い果たした

His blood carried the nutrients far through his powerful body.

彼の血液は、その強力な体を通して栄養分を遠くまで運んだ

This built strong tissues that gave him incredible endurance.

これにより、強固な組織が構築され、信じられないほどの持久力が彼に与えられました

His sight and smell became much more sensitive than before.

彼の視覚と嗅覚は以前よりもずっと敏感になりました

His hearing grew so sharp he could detect faint sounds in sleep.

彼の聴力は非常に鋭くなり、眠っている間にもかすかな音を聞き取れるようになった

He knew in his dreams whether the sounds meant safety or danger.

彼は夢の中で、その音が安全を意味するのか危険を意味するのかを知っていた

He learned to bite the ice between his toes with his teeth.

彼は足の指の間の氷を歯で噛むことを覚えた

If a water hole froze over, he would break the ice with his legs.

もし水たまりが凍ってしまったら、彼は足で氷を砕いたでしょう

He reared up and struck the ice hard with stiff front limbs.

彼は立ち上がって、硬くなった前肢で氷を強く打ち付けた

His most striking ability was predicting wind changes overnight.

彼の最も目覚ましい能力は、一晩で風の変化を予測することだった

Even when the air was still, he chose spots sheltered from wind.

空気が静止しているときでも、彼は風が当たらない場所を選んだ

Wherever he dug his nest, the next day's wind passed him by.

彼がどこに巣を掘っても、翌日の風は彼のそばを通り過ぎました

He always ended up snug and protected, to leeward of the breeze.

彼はいつも風下側の心地よい場所にいて、守られていた

Buck not only learned by experience—his instincts returned too.

バックは経験から学んだだけでなく、本能も戻りました

The habits of domesticated generations began to fall away.

家畜化された世代の習慣が消え去り始めました

In vague ways, he remembered the ancient times of his breed.

彼は漠然と、自分の種族の太古の時代を思い出した

He thought back to when wild dogs ran in packs through forests.

彼は野生の犬が群れをなして森の中を走り回っていた時代を思い出した

They had chased and killed their prey while running it down.

彼らは追いかけながら獲物を殺したのです

It was easy for Buck to learn how to fight with tooth and speed.

バックにとって、歯とスピードを使って戦う方法を学ぶのは簡単でした

He used cuts, slashes, and quick snaps just like his ancestors.

彼は先祖と同じように、カット、スラッシュ、素早いスナップを使用しました

Those ancestors stirred within him and awoke his wild nature.

それらの祖先は彼の中で揺さぶられ、彼の野性的な性質を目覚めさせた

Their old skills had passed into him through the bloodline.

彼らの古い技術は血統を通じて彼に受け継がれていた

Their tricks were his now, with no need for practice or effort.
練習も努力も必要なく、彼らの技は今や彼のものとなった

On still, cold nights, Buck lifted his nose and howled.
静かで寒い夜には、バックは鼻を上げて遠吠えしました
He howled long and deep, the way wolves had done long ago.
彼は、昔の狼がしていたように、長く深い遠吠えをした
Through him, his dead ancestors pointed their noses and howled.
彼を通して、死んだ先祖たちが鼻先を突き出して吠えた
They howled down through the centuries in his voice and shape.
彼らは彼の声と姿で何世紀にもわたって吠え続けた
His cadences were theirs, old cries that told of grief and cold.
彼の声は彼女たちの声と同じで、悲しみと寒さを物語る古い叫び声だった
They sang of darkness, of hunger, and the meaning of winter.
彼らは暗闇、飢え、そして冬の意味について歌いました
Buck proved of how life is shaped by forces beyond oneself,
バックは、人生が自分を超えた力によって形作られることを証明した
the ancient song rose through Buck and took hold of his soul.
古代の歌がバックの体内に響き渡り、彼の魂を捕らえた
He found himself because men had found gold in the North.
北で人々が金を発見したおかげで、彼は自分自身を見つけたのです
And he found himself because Manuel, the gardener's helper, needed money.
そして、庭師の助手であるマヌエルがお金を必要としていたため、彼は自分自身を見つけました

The Dominant Primordial Beast
支配的な原始の獣

The dominant primordial beast was as strong as ever in Buck.
支配的な原始の獣はバックの中で相変わらず強かった

But the dominant primordial beast had lain dormant in him.
しかし、支配的な原始の獣は彼の中に眠っていた

Trail life was harsh, but it strengthened beast inside Buck.
トレイルでの生活は過酷だったが、それがバックの内なる野獣を強くした

Secretly the beast grew stronger and stronger every day.
秘密裏に、獣は日に日に強くなっていった

But that inner growth stayed hidden to the outside world.
しかし、その内面的な成長は外の世界には隠されたままでした

A quiet and calm primordial force was building inside Buck.
静かで穏やかな原始的な力がバックの体内に形成されつつあった

New cunning gave Buck balance, calm control, and poise.
新たな狡猾さにより、バックはバランス、冷静な制御、そして落ち着きを取り戻した

Buck focused hard on adapting, never feeling fully relaxed.
バックは完全にリラックスすることなく、適応することに全力を尽くしました

He avoided conflict, never starting fights, nor seeking trouble.
彼は争いを避け、決して喧嘩を始めたり、トラブルを起こそうとしたりしなかった

A slow, steady thoughtfulness shaped Buck's every move.
ゆっくりとした着実な思慮深さがバックのあらゆる行動を形作った

He avoided rash choices and sudden, reckless decisions.
彼は軽率な選択や突然の無謀な決断を避けた

Though Buck hated Spitz deeply, he showed him no aggression.

バックはスピッツをひどく憎んでいたが、スピッツに対して攻撃的な態度は見せなかった

Buck never provoked Spitz, and kept his actions restrained.

バックはスピッツを決して刺激せず、行動を抑制した

Spitz, on the other hand, sensed the growing danger in Buck.

一方、スピッツはバックの危険が増大していることを感じ取った

He saw Buck as a threat and a serious challenge to his power.

彼はバックを脅威であり、自分の権力に対する重大な挑戦者だとみなした

He used every chance to snarl and show his sharp teeth.

彼はあらゆる機会を利用して唸り声をあげ、鋭い歯を見せた

He was trying to start the deadly fight that had to come.

彼は、これから起こるであろう致命的な戦いを始めようとしていた

Early in the trip, a fight nearly broke out between them.

旅行の初めに、彼らの間に喧嘩が起こりそうになった

But an unexpected accident stopped the fight from happening.

しかし予期せぬ事故により、戦いは中止となった

That evening they set up camp on the bitterly cold Lake Le Barge.

その夜、彼らは極寒のル・バージ湖にキャンプを設営した

The snow was falling hard, and the wind cut like a knife.

雪は激しく降り、風はナイフのように切れた

The night had come too fast, and darkness surrounded them.

夜はあっという間に来て、暗闇が彼らを包みました

They could hardly have chosen a worse place for rest.

彼らが休息のために選んだ場所は、これより悪い場所ではなかったでしょう

The dogs searched desperately for a place to lie down.
犬たちは横になれる場所を必死に探しました

A tall rock wall rose steeply behind the small group.
小さな集団の後ろには、高い岩壁がそびえ立っていました

The tent had been left behind in Dyea to lighten the load.
荷物を軽くするためにテントはダイアに残しておいた

They had no choice but to make the fire on the ice itself.
彼らには氷の上で火を起こすしか選択肢がなかった

They spread their sleeping robes directly on the frozen lake.
彼らは凍った湖の上に直接寝間着を広げました

A few sticks of driftwood gave them a little bit of fire.
流木を数本入れると、少し火がつきました

But the fire was built on the ice, and thawed through it.
しかし、火は氷の上で起こり、氷を通して溶けていきました

Eventually they were eating their supper in darkness.
結局、彼らは暗闇の中で夕食を食べていた

Buck curled up beside the rock, sheltered from the cold wind.
雄鹿は冷たい風から身を守るために岩の横で丸くなっていた

The spot was so warm and safe that Buck hated to move away.
その場所はとても暖かくて安全だったので、バックはそこから離れることを嫌がりました

But François had warmed the fish and was handing out rations.
しかしフランソワは魚を温めて食料を配っていた

Buck finished eating quickly, and returned to his bed.
バックは急いで食事を終え、ベッドに戻りました

But Spitz was now laying where Buck had made his bed.
しかしスピッツは今、バックが寝床を作った場所に横たわっていた

A low snarl warned Buck that Spitz refused to move.

低い唸り声でバックはスピッツが動くことを拒否していることを警告した

Until now, Buck had avoided this fight with Spitz.
これまで、バックはスピッツとのこの戦いを避けてきた

But deep inside Buck the beast finally broke loose.
しかし、バックの心の奥底では、ついに獣が暴走した

The theft of his sleeping place was too much to tolerate.
寝る場所を盗まれたことは耐え難いことだった

Buck launched himself at Spitz, full of anger and rage.
バックは怒りと激怒に満ちてスピッツに向かって突進した

Up until not Spitz had thought Buck was just a big dog.
これまでスピッツはバックがただの大きな犬だと思っていた

He didn't think Buck had survived through his spirit.
彼はバックが精神を通じて生き残ったとは思わなかった

He was expecting fear and cowardice, not fury and revenge.
彼は怒りや復讐ではなく、恐怖と臆病を予想していた

François stared as both dogs burst from the ruined nest.
フランソワは、2匹の犬が壊れた巣から飛び出すのを見つめた

He understood at once what had started the wild struggle.
彼はすぐにこの激しい争いの始まりが何であったかを理解した

"A-a-ah!" François cried out in support of the brown dog.
「あーあ！」フランソワは茶色の犬を応援するように叫びました

"Give him a beating! By God, punish that sneaky thief!"
「ぶちのめしてやる！神に誓って、あの卑劣な泥棒を罰せよ！」

Spitz showed equal readiness and wild eagerness to fight.
スピッツも同様の覚悟と激しい戦闘意欲を示した

He cried out in rage while circling fast, seeking an opening.
彼は怒りに叫びながら、素早く旋回し、隙を探した

Buck showed the same hunger to fight, and the same caution.

バックは、同じ戦いへの渇望と、同じ警戒心を示した

He circled his opponent as well, trying to gain the upper hand in battle.

彼はまた、戦いで優位に立とうとして、敵の周りを回りました

Then something unexpected happened and changed everything.

それから予期せぬ出来事が起こり、すべてが変わりました

That moment delayed the eventual fight for the leadership.

その瞬間が、リーダーシップをめぐる最終的な戦いを遅らせた

Many miles of trail and struggle still waited before the end.

終わりまでにはまだ何マイルもの道のりと苦労が待っていた

Perrault shouted an oath as a club smacked against bone.

棍棒が骨に打ち付けられると、ペローは罵声を浴びせた

A sharp yelp of pain followed, then chaos exploded all around.

鋭い痛みの叫び声が続き、周囲に大混乱が広がりました

Dark shapes moved in camp; wild huskies, starved and fierce.

キャンプに暗い影が動いていた飢えて獰猛な野生のハスキー犬だ

Four or five dozen huskies had sniffed the camp from far away.

4、50匹のハスキー犬が遠くからキャンプの匂いを嗅ぎ回っていた

They had crept in quietly while the two dogs fought nearby.

二匹の犬が近くで喧嘩している間に、彼らは静かに忍び寄っていた

François and Perrault charged, swinging clubs at the invaders.

フランソワとペローは侵入者に向かって棍棒を振り回しながら突撃した

The starving huskies showed teeth and fought back in frenzy.
飢えたハスキー犬たちは歯をむき出しにして狂乱して反撃した

The smell of meat and bread had driven them past all fear.
肉とパンの匂いが彼らをすべての恐怖から駆り立てた

Perrault beat a dog that had buried its head in the grub-box.
ペローは餌箱に頭を埋めていた犬を殴った

The blow hit hard, and the box flipped, food spilling out.
衝撃は強く、箱はひっくり返り、食べ物がこぼれ落ちた

In seconds, a score of wild beasts tore into the bread and meat.
数秒のうちに、数十頭の野獣がパンと肉を食い破りました

The men's clubs landed blow after blow, but no dog turned away.
男たちは棍棒で次々と打撃を与えたが、犬は一匹も逃げなかった

They howled in pain, but fought until no food remained.
彼らは痛みに叫びましたが、食べ物がなくなるまで戦いました

Meanwhile, the sled-dogs had jumped from their snowy beds.
その間に、そり犬たちは雪のベッドから飛び降りた

They were instantly attacked by the vicious hungry huskies.
彼らはすぐに凶暴な空腹のハスキー犬に襲われました

Buck had never seen such wild and starved creatures before.
バックはこれまで、このような荒々しく飢えた生き物を見たことがなかった

Their skin hung loose, barely hiding their skeletons.
彼らの皮膚は垂れ下がり、かろうじて骨格を隠しているだけだった

There was a fire in their eyes, from hunger and madness
飢えと狂気から彼らの目には炎が燃えていた

There was no stopping them; no resisting their savage rush.

彼らを止めることはできず、彼らの猛烈な突進に抵抗することもできなかった

The sled-dogs were shoved back, pressed against the cliff wall.

そり犬たちは押し戻され、崖の壁に押しつけられた

Three huskies attacked Buck at once, tearing into his flesh.

3匹のハスキー犬が一度にバックを襲い、彼の肉を引き裂いた

Blood poured from his head and shoulders, where he'd been cut.

頭と肩の切り傷からは血が流れ出た

The noise filled the camp; growling, yelps, and cries of pain.

うなり声、悲鳴、苦痛の叫びなど、騒音がキャンプに響き渡った

Billee cried loudly, as usual, caught in the fray and panic.

ビリーは騒動とパニックに巻き込まれ、いつものように大声で泣きました

Dave and Solleks stood side by side, bleeding but defiant.

デイブとソレックスは血を流しながらも反抗的に並んで立っていた

Joe fought like a demon, biting anything that came close.

ジョーは近づくものすべてに噛みつき、悪魔のように戦いました

He crushed a husky's leg with one brutal snap of his jaws.

彼は、一噛みの残忍な行為でハスキー犬の足を押し潰した

Pike jumped on the wounded husky and broke its neck instantly.

パイクは負傷したハスキー犬に飛びかかり、一瞬でその首を折った

Buck caught a husky by the throat and ripped through the vein.

バックはハスキー犬の喉を掴み、静脈を引き裂いた

Blood sprayed, and the warm taste drove Buck into a frenzy.

血が飛び散り、その温かい味がバックを狂乱させた

He hurled himself at another attacker without hesitation.
彼はためらうことなく別の襲撃者に突進した

At the same moment, sharp teeth dug into Buck's own throat.
同時に、鋭い歯がバック自身の喉に食い込んだ

Spitz had struck from the side, attacking without warning.
スピッツは警告なしに側面から攻撃した

Perrault and François had defeated the dogs stealing the food.
ペローとフランソワは食べ物を盗んでいた犬を倒した

Now they rushed to help their dogs fight back the attackers.
今、彼らは犬たちが攻撃者と戦うのを手伝うために急いで駆けつけました

The starving dogs retreated as the men swung their clubs.
男たちが棍棒を振り回すと、飢えた犬たちは退散した

Buck broke free from the attack, but the escape was brief.
バックは攻撃から逃れたが、逃走は短時間だった

The men ran to save their dogs, and the huskies swarmed again.
男たちは犬を救おうと走り、ハスキー犬たちは再び群がってきた

Billee, frightened into bravery, leapt into the pack of dogs.
ビリーは恐怖を感じながらも勇気を出して、犬の群れの中に飛び込んだ

But then he fled across the ice, in raw terror and panic.
しかし、彼は激しい恐怖とパニックに陥り、氷の上を逃げ去った

Pike and Dub followed close behind, running for their lives.
パイクとダブもすぐ後ろを追って、命からがら逃げた

The rest of the team broke and scattered, following after them.
チームの残りも散り散りになり、彼らの後を追った

Buck gathered his strength to run, but then saw a flash.
バックは逃げようと力を振り絞ったが、その時閃光を見た

Spitz lunged at Buck's side, trying to knock him to the ground.

スピッツはバックの横に突進し、彼を地面に倒そうとした

Under that mob of huskies, Buck would have had no escape.

あのハスキー犬の群れの下では、バックは逃げることができなかっただろう

But Buck stood firm and braced for the blow from Spitz.

しかしバックは毅然とした態度でスピッツの攻撃に備えた

Then he turned and ran out onto the ice with the fleeing team.

それから彼は向きを変え、逃げるチームとともに氷の上に走り出した

Later, the nine sled-dogs gathered in the shelter of the woods.

その後、9頭のそり犬たちは森の避難所に集まりました

No one chased them anymore, but they were battered and wounded.

もう誰も彼らを追いかけなかったが、彼らは打ちのめされ、傷ついた

Each dog had wounds; four or five deep cuts on every body.

どの犬にも傷があり、体には4、5箇所の深い切り傷がありました

Dub had an injured hind leg and struggled to walk now.

ダブは後ろ足を負傷し、歩くのに苦労していました

Dolly, the newest dog from Dyea, had a slashed throat.

ダイアから来たばかりの犬、ドリーの喉は切り裂かれていた

Joe had lost an eye, and Billee's ear was cut to pieces

ジョーは片目を失い、ビリーの耳は切り裂かれていた

All the dogs cried in pain and defeat through the night.

犬たちは皆、痛みと敗北感に一晩中泣き叫んでいた

At dawn they crept back to camp, sore and broken.

夜明けになると、彼らは痛みと疲労を抱えながらキャンプ地へと忍び戻った

The huskies had vanished, but the damage had been done.
ハスキー犬は姿を消したが、被害はすでにあった

Perrault and François stood in foul moods over the ruin.
ペローとフランソワは、不機嫌な気持ちで廃墟の上に立っていた

Half of the food was gone, snatched by the hungry thieves.
食べ物の半分は空腹の泥棒に奪われてしまいました

The huskies had torn through sled bindings and canvas.
ハスキー犬はそりのつなぎ目と帆布を引き裂いてしまった

Anything with a smell of food had been devoured completely.
食べ物の匂いのするものは、すべて食べ尽くされていました

They ate a pair of Perrault's moose-hide traveling boots.
彼らはペローのヘラジカ皮の旅行用ブーツを一足食べました

They chewed leather reis and ruined straps beyond use.
彼らは革のレイスを噛み砕き、ストラップを使えないほどダメにしてしまった

François stopped staring at the torn lash to check the dogs.
フランソワは引き裂かれたまつげを見つめるのをやめて、犬たちの様子を確認した

"Ah, my friends," he said, his voice low and filled with worry.
「ああ、友人たちよ」と彼は低い声で、心配そうに言った

"Maybe all these bites will turn you into mad beasts."
「この噛み傷であなたは狂った獣に変身してしまうかもしれないよ」

"Maybe all mad dogs, sacredam! What do you think, Perrault?"
「もしかしたら、みんな狂犬かもしれないよ、聖なる者よ！どう思う、ペロー？」

Perrault shook his head, eyes dark with concern and fear.
ペローは心配と恐怖で暗い目で首を振った

Four hundred miles still lay between them and Dawson.
彼らとドーソンの間にはまだ400マイルの距離があった

Dog madness now could destroy any chance of survival.
今や犬の狂気は生存の可能性をすべて破壊する恐れがある

They spent two hours swearing and trying to fix the gear.
彼らは2時間も罵りながらギアを修理しようとした

The wounded team finally left the camp, broken and defeated.
負傷したチームはついに打ちのめされ、敗北した状態でキャンプを去った

This was the hardest trail yet, and each step was painful.
これはこれまでで最も困難な道であり、一歩一歩が苦痛でした

The Thirty Mile River had not frozen, and was rushing wildly.
サーティーマイル川はまだ凍っておらず、激しく流れていた

Only in calm spots and swirling eddies did ice manage to hold.
氷は、静かな場所と渦巻く場所でのみ保持されました

Six days of hard labor passed until the thirty miles were done.
30マイルを終えるまでに6日間の重労働が続いた

Each mile of the trail brought danger and the threat of death.
道の1マイルごとに危険と死の脅威が伴いました

The men and dogs risked their lives with every painful step.
男たちと犬たちは、痛みを伴う一歩ごとに命を危険にさらした

Perrault broke through thin ice bridges a dozen different times.
ペローは薄い氷の橋を12回も突破した

He carried a pole and let it fall across the hole his body made.

彼は棒を持って、自分の体が作った穴の上にそれを落と
しました
More than once did that pole save Perrault from drowning.
その棒はペローを何度も溺死から救った
**The cold snap held firm, the air was fifty degrees below
zero.**
寒波は依然として続き、気温は零下50度だった
Every time he fell in, Perrault had to light a fire to survive.
落ちるたびに、ペローは生き残るために火を起こさなけ
ればならなかった
Wet clothing froze fast, so he dried them near blazing heat.
濡れた衣類はすぐに凍ってしまうので、炎天下で乾かし
ました
No fear ever touched Perrault, and that made him a courier.
ペローには決して恐怖心はなかった、それが彼を伝令に
したのだ
He was chosen for danger, and he met it with quiet resolve.
彼は危険に選ばれ、静かな決意でそれに立ち向かった
He pressed forward into wind, his shriveled face frostbitten.
彼はしわくちゃの顔を凍傷にしながら、風に向かって突
き進んだ
From faint dawn to nightfall, Perrault led them onward.
かすかな夜明けから夜まで、ペローは彼らを先導した
He walked on narrow rim ice that cracked with every step.
彼は、一歩ごとにひび割れる狭い氷の上を歩いた
They dared not stop—each pause risked a deadly collapse.
彼らは立ち止まることを敢えてしなかった一時停止する
たびに致命的な崩壊の危険があった
One time the sled broke through, pulling Dave and Buck in.
ある時、そりが突っ込んできて、デイブとバックを引き
ずり込んだ
By the time they were dragged free, both were near frozen.
引きずり出されても、二人とも凍り付いている状態だっ
た
The men built a fire quickly to keep Buck and Dave alive.

男たちはバックとデイブの命を救うために急いで火を起こした

The dogs were coated in ice from nose to tail, stiff as carved wood.

犬たちは鼻から尾まで氷で覆われ、彫刻された木のように硬くなっていた

The men ran them in circles near the fire to thaw their bodies.

男たちは彼らの体を解凍するために火のそばで彼らを円を描くように走らせた

They came so close to the flames that their fur was singed.

彼らは炎に非常に近づいたため、毛皮が焦げてしまいました

Spitz broke through the ice next, dragging in the team behind him.

次にスピッツが氷を突き破り、後ろのチームを引きずり込んだ

The break reached all the way up to where Buck was pulling.

ブレーキはバックが引っ張っていたところまで届きました

Buck leaned back hard, paws slipping and trembling on the edge.

バックは力強く後ろに傾き、端で足が滑り震えた

Dave also strained backward, just behind Buck on the line.

デイブもまた、ライン上のバックのすぐ後ろで後ろに力を入れました

François hauled on the sled, his muscles cracking with effort.

フランソワはそりを引っ張ったが、その努力で筋肉がポキポキと音を立てた

Another time, rim ice cracked before and behind the sled.

また別の時には、そりの前と後ろの縁の氷が割れました

They had no way out except to climb a frozen cliff wall.

彼らには凍った崖を登る以外に逃げ道がなかった

Perrault somehow climbed the wall; a miracle kept him alive.

ペローはなんとか壁を登り、奇跡的に生き延びた

François stayed below, praying for the same kind of luck.

フランソワは下に留まり、同じ幸運を祈った

They tied every strap, lashing, and trace into one long rope.

彼らは、すべてのストラップ、縛り紐、ひもを 1本の長いロープに結びました

The men hauled each dog up, one at a time to the top.

男たちは犬を一匹ずつ、頂上まで引き上げた

François climbed last, after the sled and the entire load.

フランソワはそりと荷物全体を引いて最後に登りました

Then began a long search for a path down from the cliffs.

それから崖から下る道を探す長い旅が始まりました

They finally descended using the same rope they had made.

彼らは最終的に自分たちが作ったのと同じロープを使って下山しました

Night fell as they returned to the riverbed, exhausted and sore.

彼らが疲れて痛みを抱えながら川床に戻ると、夜が明けた

They had taken a full day to cover only a quarter of a mile.

わずか4分の1マイル進むのに丸一日かかってしまった

By the time they reached the Hootalinqua, Buck was worn out.

フータリンクアに到着する頃には、バックは疲れ果てていた

The other dogs suffered just as badly from the trail conditions.

他の犬たちもトレイルの状況によって同じようにひどい苦しみを味わいました

But Perrault needed to recover time, and pushed them on each day.

しかし、ペローは時間を回復する必要があり、毎日彼らを奮い立たせました

The first day they traveled thirty miles to Big Salmon.

最初の日、彼らはビッグサーモンまで30マイル旅しました

The next day they travelled thirty-five miles to Little Salmon.

翌日、彼らはリトルサーモンまで35マイル旅した

On the third day they pushed through forty long frozen miles.

3日目に彼らは40マイルの長い凍った道を進んだ

By then, they were nearing the settlement of Five Fingers.

そのころには、彼らはファイブ・フィンガーズの集落に近づいていた

Buck's feet were softer than the hard feet of native huskies.

バックの足は、在来種のハスキー犬の硬い足よりも柔らかかった

His paws had grown tender over many civilized generations.

彼の足は、文明化されてから何世代にもわたって柔らかくなっていました

Long ago, his ancestors had been tamed by river men or hunters.

昔、彼の先祖は川の民や狩人によって飼いならされていました

Every day Buck limped in pain, walking on raw, aching paws.

バックは毎日、痛みに苦しみながら、傷ついた足を引きずりながら歩いていた

At camp, Buck dropped like a lifeless form upon the snow.

キャンプ地では、バックは雪の上に死んだように倒れていた

Though starving, Buck did not rise to eat his evening meal.

空腹であったにもかかわらず、バックは夕食を食べるために起き上がりませんでした

François brought Buck his ration, laying fish by his muzzle.

フランソワはバックの鼻先に魚を置きながら、食料を運んできた

Each night the driver rubbed Buck's feet for half an hour.

毎晩、運転手はバックの足を30分間マッサージした

François even cut up his own moccasins to make dog footwear.

フランソワは犬用の履物を作るために自分のモカシンを切り刻むことさえしました

Four warm shoes gave Buck a great and welcome relief.
4

足の暖かい靴はバックにとって大きな、ありがたい安らぎをもたらしました

One morning, François forgot the shoes, and Buck refused to rise.

ある朝、フランソワは靴を忘れてしまい、バックは起きようとしませんでした

Buck lay on his back, feet in the air, waving them pitifully.

バックは仰向けに横たわり、足を空中に上げて哀れそうに振り回していた

Even Perrault grinned at the sight of Buck's dramatic plea.

ペローでさえ、バックの劇的な嘆願を見て笑みを浮かべた

Soon Buck's feet grew hard, and the shoes could be discarded.

すぐにバックの足は硬くなり、靴は捨てられるようになりました

At Pelly, during harness time, Dolly let out a dreadful howl.

ペリーでは、ハーネスを着けている間、ドリーは恐ろしい遠吠えを上げました

The cry was long and filled with madness, shaking every dog.

その叫び声は長く、狂気に満ちており、すべての犬を震え上がらせた

Each dog bristled in fear without knowing the reason.

どの犬も理由もわからず恐怖に震えていた

Dolly had gone mad and hurled herself straight at Buck.

ドリーは気が狂って、まっすぐにバックに向かって突進した

Buck had never seen madness, but horror filled his heart.

バックは狂気を見たことがなかったが、恐怖が彼の心を満たした

With no thought, he turned and fled in absolute panic.

彼は何も考えずに、パニックに陥り、振り返って逃げ出した

Dolly chased him, her eyes wild, saliva flying from her jaws.

ドリーは目を輝かせ、口からよだれを飛ばしながら彼を追いかけました

She kept right behind Buck, never gaining and never falling back.

彼女はバックのすぐ後ろを走り続け、追いつくことも後退することもなかった

Buck ran through woods, down the island, across jagged ice.

バックは森を抜け、島を下り、ギザギザの氷の上を走った

He crossed to an island, then another, circling back to the river.

彼は一つの島へ渡り、それからまた別の島へ渡り、川へ戻っていった

Still Dolly chased him, her growl close behind at every step.

それでもドリーはうなり声をあげながら一歩一歩彼を追いかけ続けた

Buck could hear her breath and rage, though he dared not look back.

バックは彼女の息づかいや怒りの声が聞こえたが、振り返る勇気はなかった

François shouted from afar, and Buck turned toward the voice.

フランソワが遠くから叫び、バックはその声の方へ振り返った

Still gasping for air, Buck ran past, placing all hope in François.

まだ息を切らしながら、バックはフランソワにすべての希望を託して走り去った

The dog-driver raised an axe and waited as Buck flew past.

犬の御者は斧を掲げて、雄鹿が通り過ぎるのを待った

The axe came down fast and struck Dolly's head with deadly force.

斧は素早く振り下ろされ、致命的な力でドリーの頭を打ちました

Buck collapsed near the sled, wheezing and unable to move.

バックはそりの近くで倒れ、ゼーゼーと息を切らして動けなくなった

That moment gave Spitz his chance to strike an exhausted foe.

その瞬間、スピッツは疲れ切った敵を攻撃するチャンスを得た

Twice he bit Buck, ripping flesh down to the white bone.

彼はバックを二度噛み、白い骨まで肉を引き裂いた

François's whip cracked, striking Spitz with full, furious force.

フランソワの鞭が鳴り響き、猛烈な勢いでスピッツを襲った

Buck watched with joy as Spitz received his harshest beating yet.

バックはスピッツがこれまでで最もひどい殴打を受けるのを喜びながら見守った

"He's a devil, that Spitz," Perrault muttered darkly to himself.

「あのスピッツは悪魔だ」ペローは暗い声で独り言を言った

"Someday soon, that cursed dog will kill Buck—I swear it."

「近いうちに、あの呪われた犬がバックを殺すだろう誓って」

"That Buck has two devils in him," François replied with a nod.

「あのバックには悪魔が二ついるよ」フランソワはうなずきながら答えた

"When I watch Buck, I know something fierce waits in him."

「バックを見ていると、彼の中に何か恐ろしいものが待ち受けていることが分かる」

"One day, he'll get mad as fire and tear Spitz to pieces."

「ある日、彼は激怒してスピッツをバラバラに引き裂くだろう」

"He'll chew that dog up and spit him on the frozen snow."

「彼はその犬を噛み砕いて、凍った雪の上に吐き出すでしょう」

"Sure as anything, I know this deep in my bones."

「確かに、私は骨の髄までそれを知っています」

From that moment forward, the two dogs were locked in war.

その瞬間から、二匹の犬は戦い始めた

Spitz led the team and held power, but Buck challenged that.

スピッツはチームを率いて権力を握っていたが、バックはそれに挑戦した

Spitz saw his rank threatened by this odd Southland stranger.

スピッツは、この奇妙な南国の異邦人によって自分の階級が脅かされていると感じた

Buck was unlike any southern dog Spitz had known before.

バックはスピッツがこれまで知っていたどの南部の犬とも違っていた

Most of them failed—too weak to live through cold and hunger.

彼らのほとんどは失敗しました寒さと飢えに耐えるには弱すぎたのです

They died fast under labor, frost, and the slow burn of famine.

彼らは労働、寒さ、そして徐々に進行する飢餓によって急速に死んでいった

Buck stood apart—stronger, smarter, and more savage each day.

バックは際立っていた日に日に強くなり、賢くなり、そして獰猛になっていった

He thrived on hardship, growing to match the northern huskies.

彼は困難を乗り越えて、北部のハスキー犬に匹敵するほどに成長した

Buck had strength, wild skill, and a patient, deadly instinct.
バックは力強さ、優れた技術、そして忍耐強い致命的な本能を持っていました

The man with the club had beaten rashness out of Buck.
棍棒を持った男はバックから無謀さを叩き出した

Blind fury was gone, replaced by quiet cunning and control.
盲目的な怒りは消え、静かな狡猾さと制御が取って代わりました

He waited, calm and primal, watching for the right moment.
彼は落ち着いて原始的な態度で、適切な瞬間を待ちました

Their fight for command became unavoidable and clear.
彼らの指揮権をめぐる争いは避けられず、明らかになった

Buck desired leadership because his spirit demanded it.
バックは、彼の精神がリーダーシップを要求したため、リーダーシップを望んだ

He was driven by the strange pride born of trail and harness.
彼は、道と馬具から生まれた奇妙なプライドによって突き動かされていた

That pride made dogs pull till they collapsed on the snow.
そのプライドのせいで、犬たちは雪の上に倒れるまで引っ張った

Pride lured them into giving all the strength they had.
プライドが彼らを誘惑し、持てる力のすべてを捧げさせた

Pride can lure a sled-dog even to the point of death.
プライドは犬ぞりを死に至らしめることもある

Losing the harness left dogs broken and without purpose.
ハーネスを失った犬たちは、壊れて目的を失ってしまいました

The heart of a sled-dog can be crushed by shame when they retire.

そり犬は引退すると、恥ずかしさで心が押しつぶされて しまうことがあります

Dave lived by that pride as he dragged the sled from behind.
デイブはそりを後ろから引っ張りながら、その誇りを胸 に生きていた

Solleks, too, gave his all with grim strength and loyalty.
ソレックスもまた、厳しい強さと忠誠心ですべてを捧げ ました

Each morning, pride turned them from bitter to determined.
毎朝、プライドが彼らの苦々しい思いを決意に変えた

They pushed all day, then dropped silent at the camp's end.
彼らは一日中押し続け、キャンプの終わりに沈黙した

That pride gave Spitz the strength to beat shirkers into line.
その誇りがスピッツに怠け者を従わせる強さを与えた

Spitz feared Buck because Buck carried that same deep pride.
バックもスピッツと同じ強いプライドを持っていたので 、スピッツはバックを恐れていた

Buck's pride now stirred against Spitz, and he did not stop.
バックのプライドはスピッツに対して今や燃え上がり、 止まらなかった

Buck defied Spitz's power and blocked him from punishing dogs.
バックはスピッツの権力に逆らい、彼が犬を罰するのを 阻止した

When others failed, Buck stepped between them and their leader.
他の人たちが失敗したとき、バックは彼らと彼らのリー ダーの間に立ちました

He did this with intent, making his challenge open and clear.
彼は意図的にこれを実行し、自分の挑戦を公然と明確に しました

On one night heavy snow blanketed the world in deep silence.
ある夜、大雪が降り、深い静寂が世界を覆いました

The next morning, Pike, lazy as ever, did not rise for work.
翌朝、相変わらず怠け者のパイクは仕事に起きなかった

He stayed hidden in his nest beneath a thick layer of snow.
彼は厚い雪の層の下の巣の中に隠れていた

François called out and searched, but could not find the dog.
フランソワは大声で叫びながら探しましたが、犬を見つけることはできませんでした

Spitz grew furious and stormed through the snow-covered camp.
スピッツは激怒し、雪に覆われたキャンプを突撃した

He growled and sniffed, digging madly with blazing eyes.
彼はうなり声をあげ、鼻をすすり、燃えるような目で狂ったように掘り続けた

His rage was so fierce that Pike shook under the snow in fear.
彼の怒りは非常に激しく、パイクは雪の下で恐怖で震え上がった

When Pike was finally found, Spitz lunged to punish the hiding dog.
パイクがようやく見つかったとき、スピッツは隠れている犬を罰するために突進しました

But Buck sprang between them with a fury equal to Spitz's own.
しかし、バックはスピッツに匹敵する激怒で彼らの間に飛び込んだ

The attack was so sudden and clever that Spitz fell off his feet.
その攻撃はあまりにも突然で巧妙だったので、スピッツは転倒してしまった

Pike, who had been shaking, took courage from this defiance.
震えていたパイクはこの反抗に勇気を得た

He leapt on the fallen Spitz, following Buck's bold example.
彼はバックの大胆な例に倣い、倒れたスピッツに飛びかかった

Buck, no longer bound by fairness, joined the strike on Spitz.

もはや公平さに縛られなくなったバックは、スピッツへの攻撃に加わった

François, amused yet firm in discipline, swung his heavy lash.

フランソワは面白がりながらも規律を守り、重い鞭を振り回した

He struck Buck with all his strength to break up the fight.

彼は喧嘩を止めるために全力でバックを殴った

Buck refused to move and stayed atop the fallen leader.

バックは動くことを拒否し、倒れたリーダーの上に留まりました

François then used the whip's handle, hitting Buck hard.

フランソワはその後、鞭の柄を使ってバックを激しく殴った

Staggering from the blow, Buck fell back under the assault.

打撃でよろめき、バックは攻撃を受けて後ろに倒れた

François struck again and again while Spitz punished Pike.

スピッツがパイクに罰を与えている間、フランソワは何度も攻撃を続けた

Days passed, and Dawson City grew nearer and nearer.

日が経ち、ドーソン・シティはどんどん近づいてきました

Buck kept interfering, slipping between Spitz and other dogs.

バックはスピッツと他の犬の間に入り込み、邪魔をし続けました

He chose his moments well, always waiting for François to leave.

彼はタイミングをうまく選び、常にフランソワが去るのを待っていた

Buck's quiet rebellion spread, and disorder took root in the team.

バックの静かな反抗は広がり、チーム内に混乱が広がった

Dave and Solleks stayed loyal, but others grew unruly.
デイブとソレックスは忠実であり続けたが、他の者は手に負えなくなった

The team grew worse—restless, quarrelsome, and out of line.
チームはますます悪化し、落ち着きがなく、口論が激しくなり、規律が乱れるようになりました

Nothing worked smoothly anymore, and fights became common.
何もかもがスムーズにいかなくなり、喧嘩が頻繁に起こるようになりました

Buck stayed at the heart of the trouble, always provoking unrest.
バックは常に騒動の中心にいて、不安を引き起こし続けた

François stayed alert, afraid of the fight between Buck and Spitz.
フランソワはバックとスピッツの戦いを恐れて警戒を続けた

Each night, scuffles woke him, fearing the beginning finally arrived.
毎晩、乱闘で目が覚め、ついに始まりが来たのではないかと不安になった

He leapt from his robe, ready to break up the fight.
彼はローブから飛び降り、戦いを止める準備をした

But the moment never came, and they reached Dawson at last.
しかしその瞬間は来ず、彼らはついにドーソンに到着した

The team entered the town one bleak afternoon, tense and quiet.
ある荒涼とした午後、チームは緊張と静寂に包まれながら町に入った

The great battle for leadership still hung in the frozen air.

主導権をめぐる大戦争の余韻がまだ凍り付いていた

Dawson was full of men and sled-dogs, all busy with work.

ドーソンには男たちとそり犬がいっぱいいて、皆仕事に忙しそうだった

Buck watched the dogs pull loads from morning until night.

バックは朝から晩まで犬たちが荷物を引くのを見ていた

They hauled logs and firewood, freighted supplies to the mines.

彼らは丸太や薪を運び、鉱山まで物資を輸送した

Where horses once worked in the Southland, dogs now labored.

かつて南部では馬が働いていたが、今では犬が働くようになった

Buck saw some dogs from the South, but most were wolf-like huskies.

バックは南部の犬を何匹か見かけたが、ほとんどはオオカミのようなハスキー犬だった

At night, like clockwork, the dogs raised their voices in song.

夜になると、まるで時計仕掛けのように、犬たちは歌声を上げた

At nine, at midnight, and again at three, the singing began.

9時、真夜中、そして再び3時に歌が始まりました

Buck loved joining their eerie chant, wild and ancient in sound.

バックは、荒々しく古風な響きを持つ彼らの不気味な詠唱に参加するのが大好きだった

The aurora flamed, stars danced, and snow blanketed the land.

オーロラが輝き、星が踊り、大地は雪に覆われました

The dogs' song rose as a cry against silence and bitter cold.

犬の歌声は静寂と厳しい寒さに対する叫びとして響き渡った

But their howl held sorrow, not defiance, in every long note.

しかし、彼らの遠吠えの一つ一つの長い音には、反抗心ではなく悲しみが込められていた

Each wailing cry was full of pleading; the burden of life itself.
それぞれの泣き叫びは嘆願に満ちており、人生そのものの重荷でした

That song was old—older than towns, and older than fires
その歌は古い町よりも古く、火事よりも古い

That song was more ancient even than the voices of men.
その歌は人間の声よりもさらに古いものだった

It was a song from the young world, when all songs were sad.
それは、すべての歌が悲しいものだった若い世界の歌でした

The song carried sorrow from countless generations of dogs.
その歌には数え切れない世代の犬たちの悲しみが込められていた

Buck felt the melody deeply, moaning from pain rooted in the ages.
バックはそのメロディーを深く感じ、何年にもわたる痛みにうめき声をあげた

He sobbed from a grief as old as the wild blood in his veins.
彼は、自分の血管に流れる野生の血と同じくらい古い悲しみで泣きじゃくった

The cold, the dark, and the mystery touched Buck's soul.
寒さ、暗さ、そして謎がバックの魂に触れた

That song proved how far Buck had returned to his origins.
その歌はバックがいかに原点に戻ったかを証明した

Through snow and howling he had found the start of his own life.
雪と遠吠えを通して、彼は自分自身の人生の始まりを見つけた

Seven days after arriving in Dawson, they set off once again.
ドーソンに到着してから7日後、彼らは再び出発した

The team dropped from the Barracks down to the Yukon Trail.
チームは兵舎からユーコントレイルへと下りました

They began the journey back toward Dyea and Salt Water.
彼らはダイアとソルトウォーターへ戻る旅を始めました

Perrault carried dispatches even more urgent than before.
ペローは以前よりもさらに緊急な伝言を伝えた

He was also seized by trail pride and aimed to set a record.
彼はまた、トレイルでの誇りにとらわれ、記録樹立を目指しました

This time, several advantages were on Perrault's side.
今回は、ペロー側にいくつかの有利な点がありました

The dogs had rested for a full week and regained their strength.
犬たちは丸一週間休んで体力を回復しました

The trail they had broken was now hard-packed by others.
彼らが切り開いた道は、今では他の人々によって固く踏み固められていた

In places, police had stored food for dogs and men alike.
警察は場所によっては犬用と人間用の食料を備蓄していた

Perrault traveled light, moving fast with little to weigh him down.
ペローは荷物をほとんど持たずに、軽やかに、速く旅をしました

They reached Sixty-Mile, a fifty-mile run, by the first night.
彼らは初日の夜までに、50マイルの行程である60マイル地点に到達した

On the second day, they rushed up the Yukon toward Pelly.
2日目、彼らはユーコン川をペリーに向かって急いだ

But such fine progress came with much strain for François.
しかし、このような素晴らしい進歩はフランソワにとって大きな負担を伴いました

Buck's quiet rebellion had shattered the team's discipline.
バックの静かな反抗はチームの規律を崩壊させた

They no longer pulled together like one beast in the reins.
彼らはもはや、一頭の獣のように手綱を握って協力し合うことはなかった

Buck had led others into defiance through his bold example.

バックはその大胆な例によって他の人々を反抗へと導いた

Spitz's command was no longer met with fear or respect.
スピッツの命令はもはや恐怖や尊敬の対象ではなくなった

The others lost their awe of him and dared to resist his rule.
他の人々は彼に対する畏敬の念を失い、あえて彼の支配に抵抗した

One night, Pike stole half a fish and ate it under Buck's eye.
ある夜、パイクは魚を半分盗み、バックの目の下でそれを食べました

Another night, Dub and Joe fought Spitz and went unpunished.
別の夜、ダブとジョーはスピッツと戦ったが、罰せられなかった

Even Billee whined less sweetly and showed new sharpness.
ビリーも以前ほど甘く泣き言を言わなくなり、新たな鋭さを見せた

Buck snarled at Spitz every time they crossed paths.
バックはスピッツとすれ違うたびに、彼に向かって唸り声をあげた

Buck's attitude grew bold and threatening, nearly like a bully.
バックの態度は、まるでいじめっ子のように、大胆かつ威圧的なものになっていった

He paced before Spitz with a swagger, full of mocking menace.
彼は、嘲笑と脅迫に満ちた威嚇で、スピッツの前を威勢よく歩き回った

That collapse of order also spread among the sled-dogs.
その秩序の崩壊は犬ぞりの間でも広がった

They fought and argued more than ever, filling camp with noise.
彼らはこれまで以上に喧嘩や口論を繰り返し、キャンプは騒音でいっぱいになった

Camp life turned into a wild, howling chaos each night.

キャンプ生活は毎晩、騒然とした大混乱に陥った

Only Dave and Solleks remained steady and focused.
デイブとソレックスだけが落ち着いて集中力を保ってい
ました

**But even they became short-tempered from the constant
brawls.**
しかし、彼らも絶え間ない喧嘩のせいで短気になってい
ました

**François cursed in strange tongues and stomped in
frustration.**
フランソワは奇妙な言葉で罵り、苛立ちながら足を踏み
鳴らした

He tore at his hair and shouted while snow flew underfoot.
足元に雪が舞う中、彼は髪をかきむしりながら叫んだ

**His whip snapped across the pack but barely kept them in
line.**
彼の鞭は馬の群れを横切って飛んでいったが、かろうじ
て彼らを一列に並べることができた

Whenever his back was turned, the fighting broke out again.
彼が背を向けると、また戦いが始まった

François used the lash for Spitz, while Buck led the rebels.
フランソワはスピッツに鞭打ち刑を行い、一方バックは
反乱軍を率いた

Each knew the other's role, but Buck avoided any blame.
両者は互いの役割を知っていたが、バックはいかなる非
難も避けた

**François never caught Buck starting a fight or shirking his
job.**
フランソワはバックが喧嘩を始めたり仕事をさぼったり
するのを一度も見たことがなかった

**Buck worked hard in harness—the toil now thrilled his
spirit.**
バックは馬具をつけて懸命に働いたその労働が彼の心を
躍らせた

**But he found even more joy in stirring fights and chaos in
camp.**

しかし、彼はキャンプで喧嘩や混乱を引き起こすことに、さらに大きな喜びを見出しました

At the Tahkeena's mouth one evening, Dub startled a rabbit.
ある晩、タキーナ川の河口で、ダブはウサギを驚かせました

He missed the catch, and the snowshoe rabbit sprang away.
彼は捕まえ損ね、カンジキウサギは飛び去ってしまいました

In seconds, the entire sled team gave chase with wild cries.
数秒のうちに、そりのチーム全員が叫びながら追いかけました

Nearby, a Northwest Police camp housed fifty husky dogs.
近くの北西警察のキャンプには50匹のハスキー犬が飼われていた

They joined the hunt, surging down the frozen river together.
彼らは狩りに参加し、一緒に凍った川を下りました

The rabbit turned off the river, fleeing up a frozen creek bed.
ウサギは川から逸れて、凍った川床を駆け上がって逃げた

The rabbit skipped lightly over snow while the dogs struggled through.
犬たちが苦労しながら雪の上を歩いている間、ウサギは軽やかに雪の上をスキップしました

Buck led the massive pack of sixty dogs around each twisting bend.
バックは60匹の犬の大群を率いて、曲がりくねったカーブを曲がっていった

He pushed forward, low and eager, but could not gain ground.
彼は腰を低くして熱心に前進したが、前進することができなかった

His body flashed under the pale moon with each powerful leap.

力強い跳躍のたびに、彼の体は青白い月の下で光り輝いた

Ahead, the rabbit moved like a ghost, silent and too fast to catch.

前方では、ウサギが幽霊のように静かに、そして捕まえられないほど速く動いていました

All those old instincts—the hunger, the thrill—rushed through Buck.

昔からのすべての本能、飢えや興奮がバックの体を駆け巡った

Humans feel this instinct at times, driven to hunt with gun and bullet.

人間は時々この本能を感じ、銃や弾丸で狩りをしたい衝動に駆られます

But Buck felt this feeling on a deeper and more personal level.

しかし、バックはこの感情をより深く、より個人的なレベルで感じたのです

They could not feel the wild in their blood the way Buck could feel it.

彼らはバックのように血の中に野性を感じることはできなかった

He chased living meat, ready to kill with his teeth and taste blood.

彼は生きた肉を追いかけ、歯で殺して血を味わう覚悟をしていた

His body strained with joy, wanting to bathe in warm red life.

彼の体は喜びに張り詰め、温かい赤い生命を浴びたいと願っていた

A strange joy marks the highest point life can ever reach.

不思議な喜びは、人生が到達できる最高点を示します

The feeling of a peak where the living forget they are even alive.

生きている者が生きていることさえ忘れてしまうような頂上の感覚

This deep joy touches the artist lost in blazing inspiration.
この深い喜びは、燃えるようなインスピレーションに浸るアーティストの心を動かします

This joy seizes the soldier who fights wildly and spares no foe.
この喜びは、激しく戦い、敵を容赦しない兵士を捕らえます

This joy now claimed Buck as he led the pack in primal hunger.
この喜びは、原始的な飢えの中で群れを率いるバックを支配した

He howled with the ancient wolf-cry, thrilled by the living chase.
彼は生きた追跡に興奮し、古代の狼の鳴き声で遠吠えした

Buck tapped into the oldest part of himself, lost in the wild.
バックは、野生の中で失われた自分自身の最も古い部分を掘り起こしました

He reached deep within, past memory, into raw, ancient time.
彼は心の奥深く、過去の記憶、生々しい太古の時間へと到達した

A wave of pure life surged through every muscle and tendon.
純粋な生命の波がすべての筋肉と腱を駆け巡りました

Each leap shouted that he lived, that he moved through death.
それぞれの跳躍は彼が生きていること、死を乗り越えたことを叫んでいた

His body soared joyfully over still, cold land that never stirred.
彼の体は、決して動かない静かで冷たい大地の上を喜びに浮かんでいた

Spitz stayed cold and cunning, even in his wildest moments.
スピッツは、最も激しい瞬間でさえ、冷静かつ狡猾なままでした

He left the trail and crossed land where the creek curved wide.

彼は道を離れ、小川が大きく曲がっている土地を横切った

Buck, unaware of this, stayed on the rabbit's winding path.

バックはそれを知らず、ウサギの曲がりくねった道を進み続けました

Then, as Buck rounded a bend, the ghost-like rabbit was before him.

すると、バックがカーブを曲がると、幽霊のようなウサギが目の前に現れた

He saw a second figure leap from the bank ahead of the prey.

彼は獲物より先に岸から二番目の人影が飛び出すのを見た

The figure was Spitz, landing right in the path of the fleeing rabbit.

その人物は、逃げるウサギの進路上に降り立ったスピッツでした

The rabbit could not turn and met Spitz's jaws in mid-air.

ウサギは向きを変えることができず、空中でスピッツの顎にぶつかりました

The rabbit's spine broke with a shriek as sharp as a dying human's cry.

ウサギの背骨は、死にゆく人間の叫び声と同じくらい鋭い悲鳴とともに折れた

At that sound—the fall from life to death—the pack howled loud.

その音、つまり生から死への転落の音を聞いて、群れは大きな遠吠えを上げました

A savage chorus rose from behind Buck, full of dark delight.

暗い歓喜に満ちた激しい合唱がバックの後ろから上がった

Buck gave no cry, no sound, and charged straight into Spitz.

バックは叫び声も上げず、音も立てず、まっすぐスピッツに突進した

He aimed for the throat, but struck the shoulder instead.
彼は喉を狙ったが、代わりに肩を打った

They tumbled through soft snow; their bodies locked in combat.
彼らは柔らかい雪の上を転げ落ち、戦闘態勢に入った

Spitz sprang up quickly, as if never knocked down at all.
スピッツはまるで倒れたことなどなかったかのように、すぐに立ち上がった

He slashed Buck's shoulder, then leaped clear of the fight.
彼はバックの肩を切りつけ、それから戦いから逃げ去った

Twice his teeth snapped like steel traps, lips curled and fierce.
彼の歯は鋼鉄の罠のように二度カチカチと音を立て、唇は歪んで凶暴になった

He backed away slowly, seeking firm ground under his feet.
彼はゆっくりと後ずさりし、足元のしっかりした地面を探した

Buck understood the moment instantly and fully.
バックはその瞬間を即座に、そして完全に理解した

The time had come; the fight was going to be a fight to the death.
その時が来た戦いは死闘となるだろう

The two dogs circled, growling, ears flat, eyes narrowed.
二匹の犬は耳を平らにし、目を細めてうなりながら、ぐるぐる回っていました

Each dog waited for the other to show weakness or misstep.
それぞれの犬は、相手が弱みを見せたり、失敗したりするのを待っていました

To Buck, the scene felt eerily known and deeply remembered.
バックにとって、その光景は不気味なほどよく知られており、深く記憶に残っていた

The white woods, the cold earth, the battle under moonlight.
白い森、冷たい大地、月明かりの下での戦い

A heavy silence filled the land, deep and unnatural.

深く不自然な重苦しい沈黙が大地を満たした

No wind stirred, no leaf moved, no sound broke the stillness.

風も吹かず、葉も動かず、静寂を破る音もなかった

The dogs' breaths rose like smoke in the frozen, quiet air.

凍りついた静かな空気の中で、犬たちの息が煙のように立ち上った

The rabbit was long forgotten by the pack of wild beasts.

ウサギは野生動物の群れから長い間忘れ去られていました

These half-tamed wolves now stood still in a wide circle.

半分飼い慣らされた狼たちは、広い円を描いてじっと立っていました

They were quiet, only their glowing eyes revealed their hunger.

彼らは静かで、光る目だけが彼らの飢えを明らかにしていた

Their breath drifted upward, watching the final fight begin.

最後の戦いが始まるのを見ながら、彼らは息を呑んだ

To Buck, this battle was old and expected, not strange at all.

バックにとって、この戦いは古くからある予想通りのものであり、まったく奇妙なものではなかった

It felt like a memory of something always meant to happen.

それは、必ず起こるはずだった何かの思い出のように感じました

Spitz was a trained fighting dog, honed by countless wild brawls.

スピッツは数え切れないほどの野生の喧嘩によって鍛え上げられた闘犬でした

From Spitzbergen to Canada, he had mastered many foes.

スピッツベルゲンからカナダまで、彼は多くの敵を倒してきた

He was filled with fury, but never gave control to rage.

彼は激怒していたが、決して怒りを抑えることはなかった

His passion was sharp, but always tempered by hard instinct.

彼の情熱は鋭かったが、常に強固な本能によって和らげられていた

He never attacked until his own defense was in place.

彼は自分の防御が整うまで決して攻撃しなかった

Buck tried again and again to reach Spitz's vulnerable neck.

バックはスピッツの無防備な首に届くよう何度も試みた

But every strike was met by a slash from Spitz's sharp teeth.

しかし、あらゆる攻撃はスピッツの鋭い歯による斬撃に遭った

Their fangs clashed, and both dogs bled from torn lips.

彼らの牙がぶつかり合い、両方の犬の唇が裂けて血が流れた

No matter how Buck lunged, he couldn't break the defense.

バックがどれだけ突進しても、防御を破ることはできなかった

He grew more furious, rushing in with wild bursts of power.

彼はさらに激怒し、勢いよく突進した

Again and again, Buck struck for the white throat of Spitz.

バックは何度も何度もスピッツの白い喉を襲った

Each time Spitz evaded and struck back with a slicing bite.

そのたびにスピッツは回避し、切り裂くような噛みつきで反撃した

Then Buck shifted tactics, rushing as if for the throat again.

それからバックは戦術を変え、再び喉を狙うかのように突進した

But he pulled back mid-attack, turning to strike from the side.

しかし彼は攻撃の途中で後退し、横から攻撃する方向に転じた

He threw his shoulder into Spitz, aiming to knock him down.

彼はスピッツを倒すために肩をスピッツにぶつけた

Each time he tried, Spitz dodged and countered with a slash.

そのたびにスピッツはかわし、斬撃で反撃した

Buck's shoulder grew raw as Spitz leapt clear after every hit.
スピッツが攻撃するたびに飛び退くたびに、バックの肩は擦りむけてきた

Spitz had not been touched, while Buck bled from many wounds.
スピッツは傷ついていなかったが、バックは多くの傷から出血していた

Buck's breath came fast and heavy, his body slick with blood.
バックの呼吸は速くて激しくなり、彼の体は血でぬるぬるになった

The fight turned more brutal with each bite and charge.
噛みつきや突撃のたびに、戦いはより残酷なものになっていった

Around them, sixty silent dogs waited for the first to fall.
彼らの周りでは、60匹の静かにした犬たちが、最初の犬が倒れるのを待っていました

If one dog dropped, the pack were going to finish the fight.
一匹でも倒れたら、群れは戦いを終わらせるつもりだった

Spitz saw Buck weakening, and began to press the attack.
スピッツはバックが弱っているのを見て、攻撃を強め始めた

He kept Buck off balance, forcing him to fight for footing.
彼はバックのバランスを崩し、足場を確保するために戦わせた

Once Buck stumbled and fell, and all the dogs rose up.
ある時、バックがつまずいて転んだのですが、犬たちはみんな立ち上がりました

But Buck righted himself mid-fall, and everyone sank back down.
しかし、バックは落下途中で体を起こし、全員が再び地面に倒れ込んだ

Buck had something rare—imagination born from deep instinct.

バックには稀有な何かがあったそれは深い本能から生まれた想像力だ

He fought by natural drive, but he also fought with cunning.
彼は生来の衝動で戦ったが、同時に狡猾さでも戦った

He charged again as if repeating his shoulder attack trick.
彼はまるで肩攻撃の技を繰り返すかのように再び突進した

But at the last second, he dropped low and swept beneath Spitz.
しかし最後の瞬間、彼は低く身をかがめてスピッツの下をすり抜けた

His teeth locked on Spitz's front left leg with a snap.
彼の歯がスピッツの左前脚に噛みつき、パチンと音がした

Spitz now stood unsteady, his weight on only three legs.
スピッツは今や、体重を三本の足にかけただけで、不安定に立っていた

Buck struck again, tried three times to bring him down.
バックは再び攻撃し、3回も倒そうとした

On the fourth attempt he used the same move with success
4回目の試みで彼は同じ動きを成功させた

This time Buck managed to bite the right leg of Spitz.
今度はバックがスピッツの右足を噛むことに成功した

Spitz, though crippled and in agony, kept struggling to survive.
スピッツは、身体が不自由で苦しみながらも、生き残るために努力し続けました

He saw the circle of huskies tighten, tongues out, eyes glowing.
彼は、ハスキー犬の輪が狭まり、舌を出し、目を輝かせているのを見た

They waited to devour him, just as they had done to others.
彼らは、他の者たちと同じように、彼を食い尽くすのを待ちました

This time, he stood in the center; defeated and doomed.
今回、彼は敗北し、絶望の中で中心に立った

There was no option to escape for the white dog now.
白い犬にはもう逃げる選択肢はなかった

Buck showed no mercy, for mercy did not belong in the wild.
バックは慈悲を示さなかったなぜなら、慈悲は野生にはふさわしくないからだ

Buck moved carefully, setting up for the final charge.
バックは慎重に動き、最後の突撃に備えた

The circle of huskies closed in; he felt their warm breaths.
ハスキー犬の輪が近づいてきて、彼は彼らの暖かい息遣いを感じた

They crouched low, prepared to spring when the moment came.
彼らは身をかがめ、その時が来たら飛び出せるように準備した

Spitz quivered in the snow, snarling and shifting his stance.
スピッツは雪の中で震え、唸り声をあげ、姿勢を変えた

His eyes glared, lips curled, teeth flashing in desperate threat.
彼は必死に脅すように目がギラギラと輝き、唇は歪められ、歯が光っていた

He staggered, still trying to hold off the cold bite of death.
彼はよろめきながら、まだ死の冷たい痛みに耐えようとしていた

He had seen this before, but always from the winning side.
彼は以前にもこれを見たことがあったが、それは常に勝利する側からの視点だった

Now he was on the losing side; the defeated; the prey; death.
今、彼は負ける側、敗北者、獲物、そして死に瀕していた

Buck circled for the final blow, the ring of dogs pressed closer.
バックは最後の一撃を放とうと回り、犬の輪はさらに接近した

He could feel their hot breaths; ready for the kill.
彼は彼らの熱い息を感じた彼らは殺す覚悟ができていた

A stillness fell; all was in its place; time had stopped.
静寂が訪れ、すべてが整い、時間が止まった
Even the cold air between them froze for one last moment.
二人の間に漂う冷たい空気も、最後の瞬間に凍りついた
Only Spitz moved, trying to hold off his bitter end.
スピッツだけが動いて、苦しみを耐え抜こうとした
The circle of dogs was closing in around him, as was his destiny.
犬の輪が彼を取り囲み、彼の運命も迫ってきた
He was desperate now, knowing what was about to happen.
彼はこれから何が起こるかを知って、絶望していた
Buck sprang in, shoulder met shoulder one last time.
バックが飛び込んできて、最後にもう一度肩がぶつかった
The dogs surged forward, covering Spitz in the snowy dark.
犬たちはスピッツを雪の暗闇の中に包み込みながら突進した
Buck watched, standing tall; the victor in a savage world.
バックは、野蛮な世界の勝利者として、堂々と立って見守っていた
The dominant primordial beast had made its kill, and it was good.
支配的な原始の獣が獲物を仕留め、それは良かった

He, Who Has Won to Mastership
マスターの地位を獲得した者

"Eh? What did I say? I speak true when I say Buck is a devil."

「え？何だって？バックは悪魔だって言ったのは本当だ」

François said this the next morning after finding Spitz missing.

フランソワはスピッツが行方不明になっているのを発見した翌朝、こう語った

Buck stood there, covered with wounds from the vicious fight.

バックは激しい戦いで負った傷に覆われてそこに立っていた

François pulled Buck near the fire and pointed at the injuries.

フランソワはバックを火のそばに引き寄せ、怪我を指さした

"That Spitz fought like the Devik," said Perrault, eyeing the deep gashes.

「あのスピッツはデヴィクのように戦ったよ」とペローは深い切り傷を見つめながら言った

"And that Buck fought like two devils," François replied at once.

「そして、バックはまるで悪魔のように戦った」フランソワはすぐに答えた

"Now we will make good time; no more Spitz, no more trouble."

「これで順調に進むでしょうスピッツもいなくなり、トラブルもなくなります」

Perrault was packing the gear and loaded the sled with care.

ペローは用具を梱包し、そりに慎重に積み込んでいた

François harnessed the dogs in preparation for the day's run.

フランソワは、その日のランニングに備えて犬たちに馬具をつけた

Buck trotted straight to the lead position once held by Spitz.
バックは、スピッツがかつて保持していた先頭の地位までまっすぐ駆け抜けた

But François, not noticing, led Solleks forward to the front.
しかしフランソワはそれに気づかず、ソレックスを前へ導いた

In François's judgment, Solleks was now the best lead-dog.
フランソワの判断では、ソレックスが今や最高の先導犬だった

Buck sprang at Solleks in fury and drove him back in protest.
バックは激怒してソレックスに飛びかかり、抗議して彼を追い返した

He stood where Spitz once had stood, claiming the lead position.
彼はかつてスピッツが立っていた場所に立ち、トップの座を主張した

"Eh? Eh?" cried François, slapping his thighs in amusement.
「え？え？」フランソワは楽しそうに太ももを叩きながら叫んだ

"Look at Buck—he killed Spitz, now he wants to take the job!"
「バックを見てみろ、スピッツを殺したのに、今度はその仕事を奪おうとしている！」

"Go away, Chook!" he shouted, trying to drive Buck away.
「あっちへ行け、チャック！」彼はバックを追い払おうと叫んだ

But Buck refused to move and stood firm in the snow.
しかしバックは動くことを拒み、雪の中にしっかりと立ち続けた

François grabbed Buck by the scruff, dragging him aside.
フランソワはバックの首筋を掴んで、横に引きずり出した

Buck growled low and threateningly but did not attack.
雄鹿は低く威嚇するように唸ったが、攻撃はしなかった

François put Solleks back in the lead, trying to settle the dispute
フランソワはソレックスを再びリードに戻し、争いを解決しようとした
The old dog showed fear of Buck and didn't want to stay.
老犬はバックを恐れ、留まりたがりませんでした
When François turned his back, Buck drove Solleks out again.
フランソワが背を向けると、バックは再びソレックスを追い出した
Solleks did not resist and quietly stepped aside once more.
ソレックスは抵抗せず、もう一度静かに退いた
François grew angry and shouted, "By God, I fix you!"
フランソワは激怒し、「神にかけて、お前を直すぞ！」と叫びました
He came toward Buck holding a heavy club in his hand.
彼は重い棍棒を手に持ち、バックの方へ近づいてきた
Buck remembered the man in the red sweater well.
バックは赤いセーターを着た男のことをよく覚えていた
He retreated slowly, watching François, but growling deeply.
彼はフランソワを見ながら、深くうなり声を上げながらゆっくりと後退した
He did not rush back, even when Solleks stood in his place.
ソレックスが彼の代わりに立っても、彼は急いで戻りませんでした
Buck circled just beyond reach, snarling in fury and protest.
バックは怒りと抗議の唸り声を上げながら、手の届かないところを旋回した
He kept his eyes on the club, ready to dodge if François threw.
彼はフランソワがクラブを投げたら避けられるように、クラブから目を離さなかった
He had grown wise and wary in the ways of men with weapons.

彼は武器を持った男たちのやり方について賢くなり、用心深くなった

François gave up and called Buck to his former place again.
フランソワは諦めて、バックをまた元の場所へ呼びました

But Buck stepped back cautiously, refusing to obey the order.
しかしバックは慎重に後ずさりし、命令に従うことを拒否した

François followed, but Buck only retreated a few steps more.
フランソワも後を追ったが、バックはほんの数歩後退しただけだった

After some time, François threw the weapon down in frustration.
しばらくして、フランソワは苛立ちから武器を投げ捨てた

He thought Buck feared a beating and was going to come quietly.
バックは殴られるのを恐れて、静かに来るつもりだと彼は思った

But Buck wasn't avoiding punishment—he was fighting for rank.
しかし、バックは処罰を逃れていたのではなく、地位を得るために戦っていたのです

He had earned the lead-dog spot through a fight to the death
彼は死闘を繰り広げてリーダーの座を獲得した

he was not going to settle for anything less than being the leader.
彼はリーダーであること以外には満足するつもりはなかった

Perrault took a hand in the chase to help catch the rebellious Buck.
ペローは反抗的な雄鹿を捕まえるのを手伝うために追跡に加わった

Together, they ran him around the camp for nearly an hour.

二人は一緒に、彼をキャンプ場の周りで1時間近く走らせた

They hurled clubs at him, but Buck dodged each one skillfully.

彼らは彼に棍棒を投げつけたが、バックはそれを巧みにかわした

They cursed him, his ancestors, his descendants, and every hair on him.

彼らは彼と彼の先祖、彼の子孫、そして彼の髪の毛一本一本を呪った

But Buck only snarled back and stayed just out of their reach.

しかしバックは唸り声をあげるだけで、彼らの手の届かないところに留まりました

He never tried to run away but circled the camp deliberately.

彼は決して逃げようとはせず、故意にキャンプの周りを回り続けた

He made it clear he was going to obey once they gave him what he wanted.

彼は、彼らが自分の望むものをくれたら従うつもりであることを明らかにした

François finally sat down and scratched his head in frustration.

フランソワはついに座り込み、イライラしながら頭を掻いた

Perrault checked his watch, swore, and muttered about lost time.

ペローは時計を確認し、悪態をつき、失われた時間についてぶつぶつ言った

An hour had already passed when they should have been on the trail.

彼らが出発するはずだった時間には、すでに1時間が経過していた

François shrugged sheepishly at the courier, who sighed in defeat.

フランソワは、敗北感にため息をついた配達人に向かって、恥ずかしそうに肩をすくめた

Then François walked to Solleks and called out to Buck once more.

それからフランソワはソレックスのところまで歩いて行き、もう一度バックに呼びかけました

Buck laughed like a dog laughs, but kept his cautious distance.

バックは犬が笑うように笑ったが、慎重な距離を保っていた

François removed Solleks's harness and returned him to his spot.

フランソワはソレックスのハーネスを外し、彼を元の場所に戻した

The sled team stood fully harnessed, with only one spot unfilled.

そりチームはハーネスを完全に装着して立っており、空いている場所は 1 つだけでした

The lead position remained empty, clearly meant for Buck alone.

首位の座は空席のままで、明らかにバック一人の座になるはずだった

François called again, and again Buck laughed and held his ground.

フランソワは再び呼びかけたが、バックはまた笑って自分の立場を守った

"Throw down the club," Perrault ordered without hesitation.

「棍棒を投げろ」ペローはためらうことなく命令した

François obeyed, and Buck immediately trotted forward proudly.

フランソワは従い、バックはすぐに誇らしげに前へ進み出た

He laughed triumphantly and stepped into the lead position.

彼は勝ち誇ったように笑い、先頭に立った

François secured his traces, and the sled was broken loose.

フランソワは足場を固め、そりは外れた

Both men ran alongside as the team raced onto the river trail.
チームが川沿いの道を駆け抜ける間、二人は並んで走った

François had thought highly of Buck's "two devils,"
フランソワはバックの「二人の悪魔」を高く評価していた

but he soon realized he had actually underestimated the dog.
しかし、彼はすぐに、実は犬を過小評価していたことに気づいた

Buck quickly assumed leadership and performed with excellence.
バック氏はすぐにリーダーシップを発揮し、優れた成果を上げました

In judgment, quick thinking, and fast action, Buck surpassed Spitz.
判断力、素早い思考、素早い行動力において、バックはスピッツを上回った

François had never seen a dog equal to what Buck now displayed.
フランソワはバックが今見せているような犬を見たことがなかった

But Buck truly excelled in enforcing order and commanding respect.
しかし、バックは秩序を強制し、尊敬を集めることに本当に優れていました

Dave and Solleks accepted the change without concern or protest.
デイブとソレックスは、懸念や抗議もなく、その変更を受け入れました

They focused only on work and pulling hard in the reins.
彼らは仕事と手綱を強く引くことだけに集中した

They cared little who led, so long as the sled kept moving.
そりが動き続ける限り、誰が先頭に立つかはあまり気にしなかった

Billee, the cheerful one, could have led for all they cared.

明るい性格のビリーなら、どんなことでもリーダーとして活躍できただろう

What mattered to them was peace and order in the ranks.
彼らにとって重要なのは、部隊内の平和と秩序だった

The rest of the team had grown unruly during Spitz's decline.
スピッツの衰退とともに、チームの残りのメンバーも手に負えない状態になっていった

They were shocked when Buck immediately brought them to order.
バックがすぐに彼らに秩序を促したので、彼らは衝撃を受けた

Pike had always been lazy and dragging his feet behind Buck.
パイクはいつも怠け者で、バックの後ろで足を引きずっていた

But now was sharply disciplined by the new leadership.
しかし、今では新しい指導部によって厳しく規律されています

And he quickly learned to pull his weight in the team.
そして彼はすぐにチーム内で自分の役割を果たすことを学んだ

By the end of the day, Pike worked harder than ever before.
その日の終わりまでに、パイクはこれまで以上に一生懸命働きました

That night in camp, Joe, the sour dog, was finally subdued.
その晩のキャンプで、気難しい犬のジョーはようやく落ち着きました

Spitz had failed to discipline him, but Buck did not fail.
スピッツは彼を懲らしめることに失敗したが、バックは失敗しなかった

Using his greater weight, Buck overwhelmed Joe in seconds.
バックは自分の体重を利用して、数秒でジョーを圧倒しました

He bit and battered Joe until he whimpered and ceased resisting.

彼はジョーが泣き声をあげて抵抗をやめるまで、噛みつき、殴り続けた

The whole team improved from that moment on.

その瞬間からチーム全体が成長しました

The dogs regained their old unity and discipline.

犬たちは昔の団結と規律を取り戻した

At Rink Rapids, two new native huskies, Teek and Koona, joined.

リンク・ラピッズには、2匹の新しい在来種のハスキー犬、ティークとクーナが加わりました

Buck's swift training of them astonished even François.

バックの素早い訓練はフランソワさえも驚かせた

"Never was there such a dog as that Buck!" he cried in amazement.

「あのバックみたいな犬は今までいなかったよ！」彼は驚いて叫んだ

"No, never! He's worth one thousand dollars, by God!"

「いいえ、絶対にありません！彼は1000ドルの価値があるんです！」

"Eh? What do you say, Perrault?" he asked with pride.

「え？どう思う、ペロー？」彼は誇らしげに尋ねた

Perrault nodded in agreement and checked his notes.

ペローは同意してうなずき、メモを確認した

We're already ahead of schedule and gaining more each day.

すでに予定より進んでおり、日々成果が上がっています

The trail was hard-packed and smooth, with no fresh snow.

道は固く締まっていて滑らかで、新雪はありませんでした

The cold was steady, hovering at fifty below zero throughout.

寒さはずっと続き、ずっと零下50度を保っていました

The men rode and ran in turns to keep warm and make time.

男たちは暖をとり、時間を稼ぐために交代で馬に乗ったり走ったりした

The dogs ran fast with few stops, always pushing forward.
犬たちはほとんど止まることなく、常に前へ前へと速く
走り続けました

The Thirty Mile River was mostly frozen and easy to travel across.
サーティマイル川は大部分が凍っていて、渡るのは容易
でした

They went out in one day what had taken ten days coming in.
入ってくるのに10日かかったものを、彼らは1日で出か
けました

They made a sixty-mile dash from Lake Le Barge to White Horse.
彼らはレイク・ル・バージからホワイト・ホースまで60
マイルを疾走した

Across Marsh, Tagish, and Bennett Lakes they moved incredibly fast.
彼らはマーシュ湖、タギッシュ湖、ベネット湖を信じら
れないほどの速さで移動しました

The running man towed behind the sled on a rope.
走っている男はロープでそりの後ろを引っ張られていた

On the last night of week two they got to their destination.
2週目の最後の夜、彼らは目的地に到着しました

They had reached the top of White Pass together.
彼らは一緒にホワイトパスの頂上に到達した

They dropped down to sea level with Skaguay's lights below them.
彼らはスカグアイの灯りを眼下に海面まで降下した

It had been a record-setting run across miles of cold wilderness.
それは何マイルにも及ぶ寒い荒野を横断する記録的なラ
ンニングだった

For fourteen days straight, they averaged a strong forty miles.
彼らは14日間連続で平均40マイルを走りました

In Skaguay, Perrault and François moved cargo through town.

スカグアイでは、ペローとフランソワが町を通って貨物を運んだ

They were cheered and offered many drinks by admiring crowds.

彼らは称賛する群衆から歓声を浴び、たくさんの飲み物を勧められた

Dog-busters and workers gathered around the famous dog team.

有名な犬ぞりチームの周りには犬退治屋や作業員たちが集まっていた

Then western outlaws came to town and met violent defeat.

その後、西部の無法者たちが町にやって来て、激しい敗北を喫した

The people soon forgot the team and focused on new drama.

人々はすぐにそのチームのことを忘れ、新たなドラマに注目した

Then came the new orders that changed everything at once.

その後、すべてを一気に変える新たな命令が下されました

François called Buck to him and hugged him with tearful pride.

フランソワはバックを呼び寄せ、涙を浮かべながら誇りを持って抱きしめた

That moment was the last time Buck ever saw François again.

その瞬間が、バックがフランソワに再び会った最後の瞬間だった

Like many men before, both François and Perrault were gone.

以前の多くの人々と同じように、フランソワとペローの両者もいなくなっていた

A Scotch half-breed took charge of Buck and his sled dog teammates.

スコットランドの混血種がバックと彼のそり犬仲間の指揮を執った

With a dozen other dog teams, they returned along the trail to Dawson.

彼らは他の12頭の犬ぞりとともに、小道に沿ってドーソンまで戻った

It was no fast run now—just heavy toil with a heavy load each day.

今は速く走ることはできず、毎日重い荷物を背負ってただ重労働を続けているだけだ

This was the mail train, bringing word to gold hunters near the Pole.

これは、北極点付近の金採掘者に知らせを届ける郵便列車でした

Buck disliked the work but bore it well, taking pride in his effort.

バックはその仕事が嫌いだったが、自分の努力に誇りを持ってよく耐えた

Like Dave and Solleks, Buck showed devotion to every daily task.

デイブやソレックスと同様に、バックも日々のあらゆる仕事に献身的な姿勢を示しました

He made sure his teammates each pulled their fair weight.

彼はチームメイトがそれぞれ自分の役割を果たすようにした

Trail life became dull, repeated with the precision of a machine.

トレイルでの生活は機械の精度で繰り返される退屈なものとなった

Each day felt the same, one morning blending into the next.

毎日が同じように感じられ、ある朝が次の朝へと溶け合っていくようでした

At the same hour, the cooks rose to build fires and prepare food.

同じ時間に、料理人たちは起き上がり、火を起こして食事の準備をしました

After breakfast, some left camp while others harnessed the dogs.

朝食後、何人かはキャンプを出発し、他の人たちは犬に手綱をつけた

They hit the trail before the dim warning of dawn touched the sky.

夜明けの薄暗い光が空に届く前に、彼らは出発した

At night, they stopped to make camp, each man with a set duty.

夜になると、彼らは立ち止まってキャンプを設営し、各自が定められた任務を遂行した

Some pitched the tents, others cut firewood and gathered pine boughs.

ある者はテントを張り、ある者は薪を切り、松の枝を集める

Water or ice was carried back to the cooks for the evening meal.

水や氷は夕食のために料理人のもとへ運ばれました

The dogs were fed, and this was the best part of the day for them.

犬たちには餌が与えられ、それが犬たちにとって一日で一番楽しい時間でした

After eating fish, the dogs relaxed and lounged near the fire.

魚を食べた後、犬たちは火のそばでくつろぎ、くつろいでいました

There were a hundred other dogs in the convoy to mingle with.

護送隊の中には、一緒に遊べる他の犬が 100 匹ほどいました

Many of those dogs were fierce and quick to fight without warning.

それらの犬の多くは獰猛で、警告なしにすぐに戦闘を始めた

But after three wins, Buck mastered even the fiercest fighters.

しかし、3回の勝利を経て、バックは最も獰猛な戦士たちさえも打ち負かした

Now when Buck growled and showed his teeth, they stepped aside.

バックがうなり声をあげて歯をむき出すと、彼らは脇に退いた

Perhaps best of all, Buck loved lying near the flickering campfire.

おそらく何よりも、バックは揺らめくキャンプファイヤーのそばに横たわるのが大好きだった

He crouched with hind legs tucked and front legs stretched ahead.

彼は後ろ足を折り曲げ、前足を前に伸ばしてしゃがんでいました

His head was raised as he blinked softly at the glowing flames.

彼は頭を上げて、輝く炎を見つめながらそっと瞬きした

Sometimes he recalled Judge Miller's big house in Santa Clara.

彼は時々、サンタクララにあるミラー判事の大きな家を思い出す

He thought of the cement pool, of Ysabel, and the pug called Toots.

彼はセメントのプール、イザベル、そしてトゥーツという名のパグ犬のことを考えた

But more often he remembered the man with the red sweater's club.

しかし、彼は赤いセーターを着た男の棍棒のことをより頻繁に思い出した

He remembered Curly's death and his fierce battle with Spitz.

彼は縮れたの死とスピッツとの激しい戦いを思い出した

He also recalled the good food he had eaten or still dreamed of.

彼はまた、自分が食べたことのある、あるいはまだ夢に見たおいしい食べ物のことを思い出した

Buck was not homesick—the warm valley was distant and unreal.

バックはホームシックにはなっていなかった暖かい谷は遠く離れていて、非現実的だった

Memories of California no longer held any real pull over him.

カリフォルニアの思い出はもはや彼にとって何ら魅力を持たなくなっていた

Stronger than memory were instincts deep in his bloodline.

記憶よりも強かったのは、彼の血統の奥深くに宿る本能だった

Habits once lost had returned, revived by the trail and the wild.

かつて失われた習慣が、道と自然によって蘇り、戻ってきた

As Buck watched the firelight, it sometimes became something else.

バックが火の明かりを見つめていると、時々それは別のものに変わっていった

He saw in the firelight another fire, older and deeper than the present one.

彼は火の光の中に、今の火よりも古くて深いもう一つの火を見た

Beside that other fire crouched a man unlike the half-breed cook.

そのもう一つの火のそばには、混血の料理人とは違う男がうずくまっていた

This figure had short legs, long arms, and hard, knotted muscles.

この人物は短い脚と長い腕、そして硬く結びついた筋肉を持っていました

His hair was long and matted, sloping backward from the eyes.

彼の髪は長くて絡まり、目から後ろに傾いていた

He made strange sounds and stared out in fear at the darkness.

彼は奇妙な音を立て、恐怖に怯えながら暗闇を見つめて
いた

He held a stone club low, gripped tightly in his long rough
hand.

彼は石の棍棒を、長くて荒れた手でしっかりと握りしめ
、低く掲げた

The man wore little; just a charred skin that hung down his
back.

その男はほとんど何も身につけておらず、背中に焼けた
皮膚が垂れ下がっているだけだった

His body was covered with thick hair across arms, chest, and
thighs.

彼の体は腕、胸、太ももにかけて濃い毛で覆われていた

Some parts of the hair were tangled into patches of rough
fur.

毛の一部が絡まってざらざらした毛並みになっていまし
た

He did not stand straight but bent forward from the hips to
knees.

彼はまっすぐに立っていなくて、腰から膝まで前かがみ
になっていました

His steps were springy and catlike, as if always ready to
leap.

彼の足取りは弾力があって猫のようで、いつでも飛び上
がる準備ができているかのようだった

There was a sharp alertness, like he lived in constant fear.

常に恐怖の中で暮らしているかのように、鋭い警戒心が
ありました

This ancient man seemed to expect danger, whether the
danger was seen or not.

この古代人は、危険が見えるかどうかに関わらず、危険
を予期していたようでした

At times the hairy man slept by the fire, head tucked
between legs.

毛深い男は時々、足の間に頭を挟んで火のそばで眠った

His elbows rested on his knees, hands clasped above his head.

彼は肘を膝の上に置いて、両手を頭の上で組んでいた

Like a dog he used his hairy arms to shed off the falling rain.

彼は犬のように毛むくじゃらの腕を使って降り注ぐ雨を払いのけた

Beyond the firelight, Buck saw twin coals glowing in the dark.

火の明かりの向こうで、バックは暗闇の中で二つの炭が光っているのを見た

Always two by two, they were the eyes of stalking beasts of prey.

それらは常に二つずつ並んで、追跡する猛禽類の目でした

He heard bodies crash through brush and sounds made in the night.

彼は、藪を突き破って人が倒れる音や、夜に立てられた物音を聞いた

Lying on the Yukon bank, blinking, Buck dreamed by the fire.

バックはユーコン川の岸に横たわり、まばたきをしながら火のそばで夢を見ていた

The sights and sounds of that wild world made his hair stand up.

その荒々しい世界の光景と音に、彼の髪は逆立った

The fur rose along his back, his shoulders, and up his neck.

毛は背中、肩、そして首まで伸びていました

He whimpered softly or gave a low growl deep in his chest.

彼は小さくすすり泣いたり、胸の奥で低い唸り声を上げたりした

Then the half-breed cook shouted, "Hey, you Buck, wake up!"

すると混血のコックが叫んだ「おい、バック、起きろ！」

The dream world vanished, and real life returned to Buck's eyes.

夢の世界は消え去り、現実の生活がバックの目に戻った

He was going to get up, stretch, and yawn, as if woken from a nap.

彼は、まるで昼寝から目覚めたかのように、起き上がって伸びをし、あくびをするつもりだった

The trip was hard, with the mail sled dragging behind them.

郵便そりを引きずる旅は大変だった

Heavy loads and tough work wore down the dogs each long day.

重い荷物と厳しい仕事で、犬たちは長い一日を疲れ果てて過ごした

They reached Dawson thin, tired, and needing over a week's rest.

彼らは痩せて疲れ果てて、1週間以上の休息を必要とする状態でドーソンに到着した

But only two days later, they set out down the Yukon again.

しかし、わずか2日後、彼らは再びユーコン川を下って出発した

They were loaded with more letters bound for the outside world.

それらには外の世界へ送られるさらに多くの手紙が積まれていた

The dogs were exhausted and the men were complaining constantly.

犬たちは疲れ果てており、男たちは絶えず不平を言っていた

Snow fell every day, softening the trail and slowing the sleds.

雪は毎日降り、道は柔らかくなり、そりの速度は遅くなった

This made for harder pulling and more drag on the runners.

これにより、ランナーを引っ張る力が強くなり、抵抗が大きくなりました

Despite that, the drivers were fair and cared for their teams.

それにもかかわらず、ドライバーたちは公平で、チームを気遣っていました

Each night, the dogs were fed before the men got to eat.
毎晩、男たちが食事をする前に犬たちに餌が与えられました

No man slept before checking the feet of his own dog's.
自分の犬の足をチェックしないで寝る人はいません

Still, the dogs grew weaker as the miles wore on their bodies.
それでも、犬たちは長距離を走るにつれて体が弱っていった

They had traveled eighteen hundred miles through the winter.
彼らは冬の間、1800マイルを旅した

They pulled sleds across every mile of that brutal distance.
彼らはその過酷な距離を1マイルごとにそりを引いて移動した

Even the toughest sled dogs feel strain after so many miles.
最も丈夫なそり犬でも、何マイルも走ると疲れを感じます

Buck held on, kept his team working, and maintained discipline.
バックは粘り強く、チームに仕事を続けさせ、規律を保った

But Buck was tired, just like the others on the long journey.
しかし、バックは他の長旅の人たちと同じように疲れていました

Billee whimpered and cried in his sleep each night without fail.
ビリーは毎晩必ず寝ている間にすすり泣きました

Joe grew even more bitter, and Solleks stayed cold and distant.
ジョーはさらに苦々しくなり、ソレックスは冷たく距離を置いたままでした

But it was Dave who suffered the worst out of the entire team.
しかし、チーム全体の中で最も被害を受けたのはデイブでした

Something had gone wrong inside him, though no one knew what.

彼の中で何かがおかしくなったが、それが何なのか誰も知らなかった

He became moodier and snapped at others with growing anger.

彼は気分が悪くなり、怒りが増して他人に怒鳴りつけるようになった

Each night he went straight to his nest, waiting to be fed.

毎晩、彼はまっすぐ巣へ行き、餌をもらうのを待ちました

Once he was down, Dave did not get up again till morning.

一度倒れると、デイブは朝まで起き上がらなかった

On the reins, sudden jerks or starts made him cry out in pain.

手綱を引いていると、突然の衝撃や発進で馬は痛みで叫び声をあげた

His driver searched for the cause, but found no injury on him.

運転手は原因を調べたが、彼に怪我は見つからなかった

All the drivers began watching Dave and discussed his case.

ドライバー全員がデイブに注目し、彼のケースについて話し合いました

They talked at meals and during their final smoke of the day.

彼らは食事中やその日の最後の喫煙中に話をした

One night they held a meeting and brought Dave to the fire.

ある夜、彼らは会議を開き、デイブを火のそばに連れて行きました

They pressed and probed his body, and he cried out often.

彼らは彼の体を圧迫したり調べたりしたので、彼は何度も叫び声をあげた

Clearly, something was wrong, though no bones seemed broken.

骨は折れていないようだったが、明らかに何かがおかしい

By the time they reached Cassiar Bar, Dave was falling down.

彼らがカシアーバーに着いたとき、デイブは倒れていました

The Scotch half-breed called a halt and removed Dave from the team.

スコットランドの混血児は試合を中止し、デイブをチームから外した

He fastened Solleks in Dave's place, closest to the sled's front.

彼はソレックスをデイブのところ、そりの前部に一番近いところに固定した

He meant to let Dave rest and run free behind the moving sled.

彼はデイブを休ませ、動いているそりの後ろで自由に走らせるつもりだった

But even sick, Dave hated being taken from the job he had owned.

しかし、病気であっても、デイブは自分が持っていた仕事から外されることを嫌っていました

He growled and whimpered as the reins were pulled from his body.

手綱が体から引き抜かれると、彼はうなり声をあげ、すすり泣いた

When he saw Solleks in his place, he cried with broken-hearted pain.

彼は、自分の代わりにソレックスが立っているのを見て、心が痛むあまり泣いた

The pride of trail work was deep in Dave, even as death approached.

死が近づいていても、トレイルの仕事に対する誇りはデイブの中に深く残っていた

As the sled moved, Dave floundered through soft snow near the trail.

そりが進むにつれて、デイブは道の近くの柔らかい雪の上をよろめきながら進んだ

He attacked Solleks, biting and pushing him from the sled's side.

彼はソレックスを攻撃し、噛みつき、そりの横から押し出した

Dave tried to leap into the harness and reclaim his working spot.

デイブはハーネスに飛び乗って自分の作業場所を取り戻そうとしました

He yelped, whined, and cried, torn between pain and pride in labor.

彼は出産の痛みと誇りの間で引き裂かれ、わめき声を上げ、泣き言を言い、泣き叫んだ

The half-breed used his whip to try driving Dave away from the team.

混血児は鞭を使ってデイブをチームから追い出そうとした

But Dave ignored the lash, and the man couldn't strike him harder.

しかしデイブは鞭打ちを無視し、男はそれ以上強く打つことはできなかった

Dave refused the easier path behind the sled, where snow was packed.

デイブは、雪が積もったそりの後ろのより楽な道を拒否した

Instead, he struggled in the deep snow beside the trail, in misery.

その代わりに、彼は道の脇の深い雪の中で、悲惨な思いをしながらもがき続けました

Eventually, Dave collapsed, lying in the snow and howling in pain.

結局、デイブは倒れ、雪の上に横たわり、痛みに泣き叫びました

He cried out as the long train of sleds passed him one by one.

長い列のそりが次々と彼の前を通り過ぎるたびに、彼は叫びました

Still, with what strength remained, he rose and stumbled after them.

それでも、残った力を振り絞って、彼は立ち上がり、よろめきながら彼らの後を追った

He caught up when the train stopped again and found his old sled.

列車が再び止まったとき、彼は追いつき、古いそりを見つけました

He floundered past the other teams and stood beside Solleks again.

彼は他のチームを追い越して、再びソレックスの隣に立った

As the driver paused to light his pipe, Dave took his last chance.

運転手がパイプに火をつけるために立ち止まったとき、デイブは最後のチャンスをつかんだ

When the driver returned and shouted, the team didn't move forward.

運転手が戻ってきて叫んだが、チームは前進しなかった

The dogs had turned their heads, confused by the sudden stoppage.

犬たちは突然の停止に戸惑い、頭を振り返った

The driver was shocked too—the sled hadn't moved an inch forward.

運転手もショックを受けたそりは1インチも前に進んでいなかったのだ

He called out to the others to come and see what had happened.

彼は他の人たちに何が起こったのか見に来るように呼びかけた

Dave had chewed through Solleks's reins, breaking both apart.

デイブはソレックスの手綱を噛み切って、両方とも壊してしまった

Now he stood in front of the sled, back in his rightful position.

今、彼は本来の位置に戻り、そりの前に立っていました

Dave looked up at the driver, silently pleading to stay in the traces.

デイブは運転手を見上げて、車線から外れないよう静かに懇願した

The driver was puzzled, unsure of what to do for the struggling dog.

運転手は、もがいている犬をどうしたらいいのかわからず困惑した

The other men spoke of dogs who had died from being taken out.

他の男たちは、外に連れ出されて死んだ犬について話した

They told of old or injured dogs whose hearts broke when left behind.

彼らは、置き去りにされて心が張り裂けそうな老犬や怪我をした犬の話をした

They agreed it was mercy to let Dave die while still in his harness.

彼らは、デイブがハーネスをつけたまま死なせるのが慈悲であると同意した

He was fastened back onto the sled, and Dave pulled with pride.

彼はそりに再び固定され、デイブは誇らしげにそりを引っ張りました

Though he cried out at times, he worked as if pain could be ignored.

彼は時々叫び声をあげながらも、痛みを無視するかのように働き続けた

More than once he fell and was dragged before rising again.

彼は一度ならず転倒し、引きずられてから再び立ち上がった

Once, the sled rolled over him, and he limped from that moment on.

ある時、そりが彼の上を転がり落ち、彼はその時から足を引きずるようになった

Still, he worked until camp was reached, and then lay by the
fire.

それでも彼はキャンプ地に着くまで働き、その後火のそ
ばに横たわった

By morning, Dave was too weak to travel or even stand
upright.

朝になると、デイブは歩くことも、まっすぐ立つことも
できないほど衰弱していました

At harness-up time, he tried to reach his driver with
trembling effort.

馬具を装着する時間になると、彼は震える力で御者に近
づこうとした

He forced himself up, staggered, and collapsed onto the
snowy ground.

彼は無理やり起き上がり、よろめいて雪の地面に倒れ込
んだ

Using his front legs, he dragged his body toward the
harnessing area.

彼は前足を使って、ハーネスエリアに向かって体を引き
ずっていった

He hitched himself forward, inch by inch, toward the
working dogs.

彼は働く犬たちに向かって、一歩ずつ前進した

His strength gave out, but he kept moving in his last
desperate push.

彼は力が尽きたが、最後の必死の努力で動き続けた

His teammates saw him gasping in the snow, still longing to
join them.

チームメイトたちは、彼が雪の中で息を切らしながらも
、まだ彼らに加わることを切望しているのを見た

They heard him howling with sorrow as they left the camp
behind.

彼らがキャンプを後にしたとき、彼が悲しみに暮れて叫
んでいるのが聞こえた

As the team vanished into trees, Dave's cry echoed behind
them.

チームが木々の中に消えていくと、デイブの叫び声が背後で響き渡った

The sled train halted briefly after crossing a stretch of river timber.

そり列車は川沿いの林道を横切った後、しばらく停止した

The Scotch half-breed walked slowly back toward the camp behind.

スコットランドの混血児は、後ろのキャンプに向かってゆっくりと歩いていった

The men stopped speaking when they saw him leave the sled train.

男たちは彼がそり隊から去るのを見て、話すのをやめた

Then a single gunshot rang out clear and sharp across the trail.

そのとき、一発の銃声が道の向こうにはっきりと響き渡った

The man returned quickly and took up his place without a word.

男は何も言わずすぐに戻ってきて、自分の席に着いた

Whips cracked, bells jingled, and the sleds rolled on through snow.

鞭が鳴り、鈴が鳴り、そりは雪の中を進んでいった

But Buck knew what had happened—and so did every other dog.

しかし、バックは何が起こったのかを知っていました他の犬たちも同様でした

The Toil of Reins and Trail
手綱と道の苦労

Thirty days after leaving Dawson, the Salt Water Mail reached Skaguay.
ドーソンを出発してから30日後、ソルト・ウォーター・メール号はスカグアイに到着した

Buck and his teammates pulled the lead, arriving in pitiful condition.
バックと彼のチームメイトは先頭を走り、悲惨な状態で到着した

Buck had dropped from one hundred forty to one hundred fifteen pounds.
バックの体重は140ポンドから115ポンドに減っていました

The other dogs, though smaller, had lost even more body weight.
他の犬たちは、小さかったにもかかわらず、さらに体重が減っていました

Pike, once a fake limper, now dragged a truly injured leg behind him.
かつては偽の足を引きずっていたパイクは、今は本当に怪我をした足を引きずっている

Solleks was limping badly, and Dub had a wrenched shoulder blade.
ソレックスはひどく足を引きずっており、ダブは肩甲骨を捻挫していた

Every dog in the team was footsore from weeks on the frozen trail.
チームの犬たちは全員、凍った道を数週間歩き続けたため足が痛かった

They had no spring left in their steps, only slow, dragging motion.
彼らの足取りにはもう弾力はなく、ただゆっくりと、引きずるように動いているだけだった

Their feet hit the trail hard, each step adding more strain to their bodies.

彼らの足は道を強く踏みしめ、一歩ごとに彼らの体にかかる負担は増していった

They were not sick, only drained beyond all natural recovery.

彼らは病気だったわけではなく、ただ自然治癒できないほど衰弱していただけだった

This was not tiredness from one hard day, cured with a night's rest.

これは、一晩休めば治る、一日のハードな疲れではありませんでした

It was exhaustion built slowly through months of grueling effort.

それは何ヶ月にもわたる厳しい努力によって徐々に蓄積された疲労でした

No reserve strength remained—they had used up every bit they had.

予備兵力は残っていなかった——彼らは持てる力をすべて使い果たしてしまったのだ

Every muscle, fiber, and cell in their bodies was spent and worn.

彼らの体のあらゆる筋肉、繊維、細胞は消耗し、すり減っていました

And there was a reason—they had covered twenty-five hundred miles.

そして、それには理由があった彼らは2500マイルもの距離を移動していたのだ

They had rested only five days during the last eighteen hundred miles.

彼らは最後の1800マイルの間にたった5日間しか休んでいなかった

When they reached Skaguay, they looked barely able to stand upright.

スカグアイに到着したとき、彼らはほとんど直立できない状態だった

They struggled to keep the reins tight and stay ahead of the sled.

彼らは手綱をしっかり握ってそりより前に出ようと奮闘した

On downhill slopes, they only managed to avoid being run over.

下り坂では、彼らは轢かれるのをなんとか避けることができた

"March on, poor sore feet," the driver said as they limped along.

「痛む足よ、進め、哀れな者たちよ」と、運転手は足を引きずりながら言った

"This is the last stretch, then we all get one long rest, for sure."

「これが最後の区間ですその後は必ず全員長い休息が取れます」

"One truly long rest," he promised, watching them stagger forward.

「本当に長い休息だ」と彼は彼らがよろめきながら前進するのを見ながら約束した

The drivers expected they were going to now get a long, needed break.

ドライバーたちは、これから長く必要な休憩が取れるだろうと期待していた

They had traveled twelve hundred miles with only two days' rest.

彼らはたった二日間の休息で1200マイルも旅した

By fairness and reason, they felt they had earned time to relax.

公平さと理性から判断して、彼らはリラックスする時間を得たと感じました

But too many had come to the Klondike, and too few had stayed home.

しかし、クロンダイクに来た人は多すぎ、家に残った人は少なすぎた

Letters from families flooded in, creating piles of delayed mail.

家族からの手紙が殺到し、遅延した郵便物が山積みになった

Official orders arrived—new Hudson Bay dogs were going to take over.

正式な命令が届き、新しいハドソン湾犬が引き継ぐことになった

The exhausted dogs, now called worthless, were to be disposed of.

疲れ果てた犬たちは、今では価値がないとみなされ、処分されることになりました

Since money mattered more than dogs, they were going to be sold cheaply.

犬よりもお金の方が大切だったので、犬は安く売られることになった

Three more days passed before the dogs felt just how weak they were.

犬たちが自分たちがどれほど弱っているかを実感するまで、さらに3日が経過しました

On the fourth morning, two men from the States bought the whole team.

4日目の朝、アメリカ人の男性2人がチーム全員を購入しました

The sale included all the dogs, plus their worn harness gear.

販売対象には犬全員と、使い古したハーネスも含まれていた

The men called each other "Hal" and "Charles" as they completed the deal.

取引を終えると、二人は互いを「ハル」と「チャールズ」と呼び合った

Charles was middle-aged, pale, with limp lips and fierce mustache tips.

チャールズは中年で、青白く、唇は弱々しく、口ひげの先端は鋭かった

Hal was a young man, maybe nineteen, wearing a cartridge-stuffed belt.

ハルは、弾薬を詰めたベルトを締めている、おそらく19歳くらいの若者だった

The belt held a big revolver and a hunting knife, both unused.

ベルトには大きなリボルバーと狩猟用ナイフが入っていたが、どちらも使われていなかった

It showed how inexperienced and unfit he was for northern life.

それは彼が北部の生活にいかに経験不足で不向きであるかを示していた

Neither man belonged in the wild; their presence defied all reason.

どちらの男も荒野には属していなかった彼らの存在はあらゆる理性を無視していた

Buck watched as money exchanged hands between buyer and agent.

バックは買い手とエージェントの間でお金がやり取りされるのを見ていた

He knew the mail-train drivers were leaving his life like the rest.

彼は、郵便列車の運転手たちが他の人々と同じように彼の人生から去っていくことを知っていた

They followed Perrault and François, now gone beyond recall.

彼らは、今ではもう呼び戻すことのできないペローとフランソワの後を追った

Buck and the team were led to their new owners' sloppy camp.

バックとチームは新しいオーナーの雑然としたキャンプに連れて行かれた

The tent sagged, dishes were dirty, and everything lay in disarray.

テントはたわみ、食器は汚れ、すべてが乱雑に放置されていました

Buck noticed a woman there too—Mercedes, Charles's wife and Hal's sister.

バックはそこにいる女性にも気づいたメルセデス、チャールズの妻でありハルの妹だった

They made a complete family, though far from suited to the trail.

彼らはトレイルにはまったく適していなかったが、完璧な家族だった

Buck watched nervously as the trio started packing the supplies.

バックは、3人が荷物を詰め始めるのを不安そうに見守っていた

They worked hard but without order—just fuss and wasted effort.

彼らは一生懸命働きましたが、秩序がなく、ただ騒ぎ立てて無駄な努力をしました

The tent was rolled into a bulky shape, far too large for the sled.

テントはかさばる形に丸められており、そりには大きすぎました

Dirty dishes were packed without being cleaned or dried at all.

汚れた食器は全く洗浄も乾燥もされずに梱包されていました

Mercedes fluttered about, constantly talking, correcting, and meddling.

メルセデスは、あちこち飛び回りながら、絶えず話しかけたり、訂正したり、干渉したりしていた

When a sack was placed on front, she insisted it go on the back.

袋が前に置かれると、彼女はそれを後ろに置くよう主張しました

She packed the sack in the bottom, and the next moment she needed it.

彼女は袋の底に荷物を詰め込み、次の瞬間にはそれが必要になった

So the sled was unpacked again to reach the one specific
bag.
そこで、特定のバッグに到達するために、そりを再度開
梱しました

Nearby, three men stood outside a tent, watching the scene
unfold.
近くでは、3人の男がテントの外に立って、その光景を
見守っていた

They smiled, winked, and grinned at the newcomers'
obvious confusion.
彼らは新参者の明らかな困惑に微笑み、ウインクし、ニ
ヤリと笑った

"You've got a right heavy load already," said one of the men.
「もうかなり重い荷物を背負っているね」と男の一人が
言った

"I don't think you should carry that tent, but it's your
choice."
「そのテントを運ぶべきではないと思うが、それはあな
たの選択だ」

"Undreamed of!" cried Mercedes, throwing up her hands in
despair.
「夢にも思わなかった！」メルセデスは絶望して両手を
上げて叫んだ

"How could I possibly travel without a tent to stay under?"
「寝るためのテントなしでどうやって旅行できるの？」

"It's springtime—you won't see cold weather again," the
man replied.
「春だよもう寒い天気は来ないよ」と男は答えた

But she shook her head, and they kept piling items onto the
sled.
しかし彼女は首を横に振り、彼らはそりに荷物を積み続
けました

The load towered dangerously high as they added the final
things.
最後の荷物を追加すると、荷物は危険なほど高くなりま
した

"Think the sled will ride?" asked one of the men with a skeptical look.

「そりは滑ると思いますか？」と男性の一人が疑わしげな表情で尋ねた

"Why shouldn't it?" Charles snapped back with sharp annoyance.

「なぜダメなんだ？」チャールズは激しく苛立ちながら言い返した

"Oh, that's all right," the man said quickly, backing away from offense.

「ああ、大丈夫ですよ」男は攻撃的な態度を避けながら、すぐに言った

"I was only wondering—it just looked a bit too top-heavy to me."

「ただ気になっただけですちょっとトップヘビーすぎるように見えたんです」

Charles turned away and tied down the load as best as he could.

チャールズは向きを変えて、できる限り荷物を縛り付けた

But the lashings were loose and the packing poorly done overall.

しかし、縛りが緩んでおり、梱包も全体的に不十分でした

"Sure, the dogs will pull that all day," another man said sarcastically.

「確かに、犬たちは一日中それを引っ張るだろうね」と別の男性が皮肉っぽく言った

"Of course," Hal replied coldly, grabbing the sled's long gee-pole.

「もちろんだ」ハルはそりの長いジーポールを掴みながら冷たく答えた

With one hand on the pole, he swung the whip in the other.

彼は片手で棒を持ち、もう一方の手で鞭を振り回した

"Let's go!" he shouted. "Move it!" urging the dogs to start.

「行くぞ！」と彼は叫んだ「進め！」犬たちに出発を促した

The dogs leaned into the harness and strained for a few moments.

犬たちはハーネスに寄りかかり、しばらく力を入れていました

Then they stopped, unable to budge the overloaded sled an inch.

そして彼らは立ち止まり、荷物を積みすぎたそりを1インチも動かすことができなかった

"The lazy brutes!" Hal yelled, lifting the whip to strike them.

「怠け者の獣どもめ！」ハルは鞭を振り上げて奴らを殴りつけながら叫んだ

But Mercedes rushed in and seized the whip from Hal's hands.

しかしメルセデスが駆け寄ってきてハルの手から鞭を奪い取った

"Oh, Hal, don't you dare hurt them," she cried in alarm.

「ああ、ハル、彼らを傷つけないで」彼女は驚いて叫んだ

"Promise me you'll be kind to them, or I won't go another step."

「彼らに優しくすると約束してくださいそうしないと私はもう一歩も進めません」

"You don't know a thing about dogs," Hal snapped at his sister.

「君は犬のことを何も知らないね」ハルは妹に言い放った

"They're lazy, and the only way to move them is to whip them."

「彼らは怠け者なので、彼らを動かすには鞭打つしかないのです」

"Ask anyone—ask one of those men over there if you doubt me."

「誰に聞いても構いません私を疑うなら、あそこにいる男の人に聞いてみてください」

Mercedes looked at the onlookers with pleading, tearful eyes.

メルセデスは涙に濡れた目で懇願するような目で見物人たちを見つめた

Her face showed how deeply she hated the sight of any pain.

彼女の顔を見れば、どんな痛みを見るのもどれほど嫌っているかがわかった

"They're weak, that's all," one man said. "They're worn out."

「ただ弱っているだけだ」とある男性は言った「疲れ切っているんだ」

"They need rest—they've been worked too long without a break."

「彼らには休息が必要です休みなく長時間働きすぎているのです」

"Rest be cursed," Hal muttered with his lip curled.

「呪われろ」ハルは唇を歪めて呟いた

Mercedes gasped, clearly pained by the coarse word from him.

メルセデスは、彼のひどい言葉に明らかに傷つき、息を呑んだ

Still, she stayed loyal and instantly defended her brother.

それでも彼女は忠誠を貫き、即座に兄を擁護した

"Don't mind that man," she said to Hal. "They're our dogs."

「あの男のことは気にしないで」と彼女はハルに言った「あの人たちは私たちの犬よ」

"You drive them as you see fit—do what you think is right."

「あなたは自分が適切だと思うように運転しますあなたが正しいと思うことをしてください」

Hal raised the whip and struck the dogs again without mercy.

ハルは鞭を振り上げ、容赦なく再び犬たちを叩いた

They lunged forward, bodies low, feet pushing into the snow.

彼らは体を低くし、足を雪の中に押し付けながら前方に突進した

All their strength went into the pull, but the sled wasn't moving.

全員の力を込めてそりを引っ張ったが、そりは動かなかった

The sled stayed stuck, like an anchor frozen into the packed snow.

そりは、固まった雪の中に凍りついた錨のように動けなくなった

After a second effort, the dogs stopped again, panting hard.

二度目の努力の後、犬たちは激しく息を切らしながら再び立ち止まりました

Hal raised the whip once more, just as Mercedes interfered again.

ハルは再び鞭を振り上げたが、そのときメルセデスがまたもや介入した

She dropped to her knees in front of Buck and hugged his neck.

彼女はバックの前でひざまずき、彼の首を抱きしめた

Tears filled her eyes as she pleaded with the exhausted dog.

疲れ果てた犬に懇願する彼女の目には涙が溢れていた

"You poor dears," she said, "why don't you just pull harder?"

「かわいそうに」と彼女は言った「もっと強く引っ張ったらどう?」

"If you pull, then you won't get to be whipped like this."

「引っ張ったら、こんな風に鞭打たれちゃ駄目だよ」

Buck disliked Mercedes, but he was too tired to resist her now.

バックはメルセデスが嫌いだったが、今は疲れすぎて彼女に抵抗できなかった

He accepted her tears as just another part of the miserable day.

彼は彼女の涙を、その悲惨な一日の出来事として受け止めた

One of the watching men finally spoke after holding back his anger.

見ていた男の一人が、怒りを抑えてようやく口を開いた

"I don't care what happens to you folks, but those dogs matter."

「あなたたちに何が起ころうと構わないが、あの犬たちは大事だ」

"If you want to help, break that sled loose—it's frozen to the snow."

「助けたいなら、そりを解いてください雪に凍り付いていますよ」

"Push hard on the gee-pole, right and left, and break the ice seal."

「ジーポールを左右に強く押して、氷の封印を破ってください」

A third attempt was made, this time following the man's suggestion.

3度目の試みは、今度は男性の提案に従って行われた

Hal rocked the sled from side to side, breaking the runners loose.

ハルはそりを左右に揺らして、ランナーを外した

The sled, though overloaded and awkward, finally lurched forward.

そりは、荷物を積みすぎて不格好だったが、ついによろめきながら前進した

Buck and the others pulled wildly, driven by a storm of whiplashes.

バックと他の者たちは、むち打ちの嵐に駆られて、激しく引っ張った

A hundred yards ahead, the trail curved and sloped into the street.

100ヤードほど進むと、道はカーブして道路へと続いていました

It was going to have taken a skilled driver to keep the sled upright.

そりをまっすぐに保つには熟練した運転手が必要だった
だろう

Hal was not skilled, and the sled tipped as it swung around
the bend.

ハルは熟練していなかったので、そりはカーブを曲がる
ときに傾いてしまいました

Loose lashings gave way, and half the load spilled onto the
snow.

緩んだ縛りが崩れ、荷物の半分が雪の上にこぼれ落ちた

The dogs did not stop; the lighter sled flew along on its side.

犬たちは止まらず、軽いそりは横向きに進んでいった

Angry from abuse and the heavy burden, the dogs ran faster.

虐待と重い荷物に怒った犬たちは、さらに速く走りまし
た

Buck, in fury, broke into a run, with the team following
behind.

バックは激怒して走り出し、チームはその後を追った

Hal shouted "Whoa! Whoa!" but the team paid no attention
to him.

ハルは「うわっ！うわっ！」と叫んだが、チームは彼に
注意を払わなかった

He tripped, fell, and was dragged along the ground by the
harness.

彼はつまずいて転倒し、ハーネスによって地面に引きず
られました

The overturned sled bumped over him as the dogs raced on
ahead.

犬たちが先を走り去る中、ひっくり返ったそりが彼の上
を転がり落ちた

The rest of the supplies scattered across Skaguay's busy
street.

残りの物資はスカグアイの賑やかな通りに散らばってい
た

Kind-hearted people rushed to stop the dogs and gather the
gear.

心優しい人々が急いで犬を止め、道具を集めました

They also gave advice, blunt and practical, to the new travelers.

彼らはまた、新しい旅行者に率直かつ実践的なアドバイスを与えました

"If you want to reach Dawson, take half the load and double the dogs."

「ドーソンに着きたいなら、荷物を半分にして犬を倍にしてください」

Hal, Charles, and Mercedes listened, though not with enthusiasm.

ハル、チャールズ、メルセデスは熱心ではなかったものの、耳を傾けた

They pitched their tent and started sorting through their supplies.

彼らはテントを張り、物資を整理し始めた

Out came canned goods, which made onlookers laugh aloud.

缶詰が出てきて、見物人は大笑いした

"Canned stuff on the trail? You'll starve before that melts," one said.

「道に缶詰があるなんて？溶ける前に餓死しちゃうよ」と、ある人は言った

"Hotel blankets? You're better off throwing them all out."

「ホテルの毛布？全部捨てた方がいいですよ」

"Ditch the tent, too, and no one washes dishes here."

「テントも撤去したら、ここで皿を洗う人は誰もいなくなるよ」

"You think you're riding a Pullman train with servants on board?"

「あなたは、乗客が乗っているプルマン列車に乗っていると思っているのですか？」

The process began—every useless item was tossed to the side.

プロセスが始まりました役に立たないアイテムはすべて脇に投げ捨てられました

Mercedes cried when her bags were emptied onto the snowy ground.

メルセデスは、バッグの中身が雪の地面に空けられたとき、泣きました

She sobbed over every item thrown out, one by one without pause.

彼女は、投げ出された品物の一つ一つを見つめながら、休むことなく泣き続けた

She vowed not to go one more step—not even for ten Charleses.

彼女はもう一歩も進まないと誓ったたとえ10チャールズでも

She begged each person nearby to let her keep her precious things.

彼女は近くにいる人一人一人に、大切なものを預けてくれるよう頼みました

At last, she wiped her eyes and began tossing even vital clothes.

ついに彼女は目を拭いて、大切な服さえも投げ捨て始めた

When done with her own, she began emptying the men's supplies.

自分のものを片付け終わると、彼女は男性用のものを空にし始めた

Like a whirlwind, she tore through Charles and Hal's belongings.

彼女はまるで旋風のようにチャールズとハルの持ち物を破壊した

Though the load was halved, it was still far heavier than needed.

荷物は半分になったが、それでもまだ必要以上に重かった

That night, Charles and Hal went out and bought six new dogs.

その夜、チャールズとハルは出かけて6匹の新しい犬を買いました

These new dogs joined the original six, plus Teek and Koona.

これらの新しい犬は、元々の 6
匹と、ティークとクーナに加わりました

Together they made a team of fourteen dogs hitched to the sled.

彼らは一緒に、そりに繋がれた14匹の犬のチームを結成しました

But the new dogs were unfit and poorly trained for sled work.

しかし、新しい犬たちはそり遊びには不向きで、十分な訓練も受けていませんでした

Three of the dogs were short-haired pointers, and one was a Newfoundland.

犬のうち3匹は短毛ポインターで、1匹はニューファンドランドでした

The final two dogs were mutts of no clear breed or purpose at all.

最後の2匹の犬は、品種も用途もまったくわからない雑種犬でした

They didn't understand the trail, and they didn't learn it quickly.

彼らは道を理解しておらず、すぐに習得することもできませんでした

Buck and his mates watched them with scorn and deep irritation.

バックとその仲間たちは軽蔑と強い苛立ちの気持ちで彼らを見ていた

Though Buck taught them what not to do, he could not teach duty.

バックは彼らに何をしてはいけないかを教えたが、義務を教える事はできなかった

They didn't take well to trail life or the pull of reins and sleds.

彼らは、山道を歩く生活や手綱やそりの引くことにあまり慣れていなかった

Only the mongrels tried to adapt, and even they lacked fighting spirit.

適応しようとしたのは雑種犬だけだったが、彼らにさえ
闘志が欠けていた

The other dogs were confused, weakened, and broken by
their new life.

他の犬たちは新しい生活に混乱し、弱り果て、打ちのめ
されました

With the new dogs clueless and the old ones exhausted,
hope was thin.

新しい犬たちは何も分からず、古い犬たちは疲れ果てて
いたので、希望は薄かった

Buck's team had covered twenty-five hundred miles of harsh
trail.

バックのチームは2500マイルの厳しい道を歩いた

Still, the two men were cheerful and proud of their large dog
team.

それでも、二人の男は明るく、自分たちの大型犬チーム
を誇りに思っていた

They thought they were traveling in style, with fourteen
dogs hitched.

彼らは14匹の犬を連れて優雅に旅をしていると思ってい
た

They had seen sleds leave for Dawson, and others arrive
from it.

彼らは、ドーソンに向けて出発するそりや、そこから到
着するそりを見た

But never had they seen one pulled by as many as fourteen
dogs.

しかし、14匹もの犬に引かれる馬は見たことがなかった

There was a reason such teams were rare in the Arctic
wilderness.

北極の荒野でそのようなチームが珍しいのには理由があ
りました

No sled could carry enough food to feed fourteen dogs for
the trip.

旅の間、14匹の犬に食べさせるのに十分な食料を運ぶこ
とのできるそりはなかった

But Charles and Hal didn't know that—they had done the math.

しかし、チャールズとハルはそれを知らなかった——彼らは計算していたのだ

They penciled out the food: so much per dog, so many days, done.

彼らは餌の量を計算しました犬1匹につきこれだけの量、何日分、これで完了です

Mercedes looked at their figures and nodded as if it made sense.

メルセデスは彼らの姿を見て、納得したかのようにうなずいた

It all seemed very simple to her, at least on paper.

少なくとも書類の上では、彼女にとってはすべてが非常に単純に思えた

The next morning, Buck led the team slowly up the snowy street.

翌朝、バックは一行を率いて雪の積もった道をゆっくりと登っていった

There was no energy or spirit in him or the dogs behind him.

彼にも、彼の後ろにいる犬たちにも、エネルギーも気力もありませんでした

They were dead tired from the start—there was no reserve left.

彼らは最初からひどく疲れていて、余力は残っていませんでした

Buck had made four trips between Salt Water and Dawson already.

バックはすでにソルトウォーターとドーソンの間を4回往復していた

Now, faced with the same trail again, he felt nothing but bitterness.

今、再び同じ道に直面して、彼はただ苦々しい思いしか感じなかった

His heart was not in it, nor were the hearts of the other dogs.
彼の心はそこになかったし、他の犬たちの心もそこにな
かった
The new dogs were timid, and the huskies lacked all trust.
新しい犬たちは臆病で、ハスキー犬たちは全く信頼を寄
せていなかった
Buck sensed he could not rely on these two men or their
sister.
バックは、この二人の男やその妹には頼れないと感じた
They knew nothing and showed no signs of learning on the
trail.
彼らは何も知らず、道中で学ぶ気配も見せなかった
They were disorganized and lacked any sense of discipline.
彼らは無秩序であり、規律感覚が欠如していました
It took them half the night to set up a sloppy camp each
time.
毎回、雑なキャンプを設営するのに半夜かかりました
And half the next morning they spent fumbling with the
sled again.
そして彼らは翌朝の半分を再びそりをいじくり回しなが
ら過ごした
By noon, they often stopped just to fix the uneven load.
正午になると、荷物の不均等を修正するためだけに作業
が止まることもよくありました
On some days, they traveled less than ten miles in total.
ある日には、合計で10マイル未満しか移動しませんでし
た
Other days, they didn't manage to leave camp at all.
他の日には、キャンプからまったく出られなかった
They never came close to covering the planned food-
distance.
彼らは計画していた食料調達距離をカバーすることに決
して近づきませんでした
As expected, they ran short on food for the dogs very
quickly.
予想通り、犬の餌はすぐに足りなくなってしまいました

They made matters worse by overfeeding in the early days.
彼らは初期の頃に餌を与えすぎたために事態を悪化させました

This brought starvation closer with every careless ration.
こうすると、不注意な配給のたびに飢餓が近づいていった

The new dogs had not learned to survive on very little.
新しい犬たちは、ほんのわずかなもので生き延びることを学んでいなかった

They ate hungrily, with appetites too large for the trail.
彼らは道中、空腹のまま食べ続けた

Seeing the dogs weaken, Hal believed the food wasn't enough.
犬たちが弱っていくのを見て、ハルは食べ物が十分ではなかったと考えた

He doubled the rations, making the mistake even worse.
彼は食料を倍増させたが、その結果、間違いはさらに悪化した

Mercedes added to the problem with tears and soft pleading.
メルセデスは涙と優しい嘆願で問題をさらに悪化させた

When she couldn't convince Hal, she fed the dogs in secret.
ハルを説得できなかったので、彼女はこっそりと犬たちに餌を与えた

She stole from the fish sacks and gave it to them behind his back.
彼女は魚袋から盗み、彼に内緒で彼らにそれを渡した

But what the dogs truly needed wasn't more food—it was rest.
しかし、犬たちが本当に必要としていたのは、より多くの食べ物ではなく、休息でした

They were making poor time, but the heavy sled still dragged on.
彼らの進みは遅かったが、重いそりは依然として引きずりながら進んでいった

That weight alone drained their remaining strength each day.

その重さだけで、彼らの残りの体力は毎日消耗していきました

Then came the stage of underfeeding as the supplies ran low.
その後、食料が不足し、給餌不足の段階になりました

Hal realized one morning that half the dog food was already gone.
ある朝、ハルはドッグフードがすでに半分なくなっていることに気づきました

They had only traveled a quarter of the total trail distance.
彼らはトレイルの総距離の4分の1しか歩いていなかった

No more food could be bought, no matter what price was offered.
いくら値段をつけても、もう食べ物を買うことはできなかった

He reduced the dogs' portions below the standard daily ration.
彼は犬への餌の量を標準的な1日の配給量よりも減らした

At the same time, he demanded longer travel to make up for loss.
同時に、彼は損失を補うためにさらに長い旅程を要求した

Mercedes and Charles supported this plan, but failed in execution.
メルセデスとチャールズはこの計画を支持したが、実行には失敗した

Their heavy sled and lack of skill made progress nearly impossible.
彼らのそりは重く、技術も不足していたため、前進することはほとんど不可能でした

It was easy to give less food, but impossible to force more effort.
食べ物を減らすのは簡単でしたが、さらに努力を強制することは不可能でした

They couldn't start early, nor could they travel for extra hours.

早く出発することも、長時間移動することもできませんでした

They didn't know how to work the dogs, nor themselves, for that matter.

彼らは犬をどう扱えばいいのか知らなかったし、実際のところ、自分自身のことも知らなかった

The first dog to die was Dub, the unlucky but hardworking thief.

最初に死んだ犬は、不運ではあるが働き者の泥棒、ダブでした

Though often punished, Dub had pulled his weight without complaint.

ダブは何度も罰せられたが、文句も言わず自分の役割を果たしてきた

His injured shoulder grew worse without care or needed rest.

適切な治療も休息も受けなかったため、負傷した肩は悪化していった

Finally, Hal used the revolver to end Dub's suffering.

ついにハルはリボルバーを使いダブの苦しみを終わらせた

A common saying claimed that normal dogs die on husky rations.

よく言われるように、普通の犬はハスキー犬用の餌を与えると死んでしまうそうです

Buck's six new companions had only half the husky's share of food.

バックの新しい仲間6匹は、ハスキーの半分の量の食べ物しか食べられなかった

The Newfoundland died first, then the three short-haired pointers.

最初にニューファンドランドが死亡し、続いて3匹のショートヘアード・ポインターが死亡した

The two mongrels held on longer but finally perished like the rest.

二匹の雑種犬は長く持ちこたえましたが、最終的には他の犬たちと同じように死んでしまいました

By this time, all the amenities and gentleness of the Southland were gone.

この時までに、サウスランドの快適さと穏やかさはすべて失われていました

The three people had shed the last traces of their civilized upbringing.

三人は文明的な育ちの最後の痕跡を捨て去った

Stripped of glamour and romance, Arctic travel became brutally real.

魅力とロマンが削ぎ落とされ、北極旅行は残酷な現実となった

It was a reality too harsh for their sense of manhood and womanhood.

それは彼らの男らしさ、女らしさの感覚にとってあまりに厳しい現実だった

Mercedes no longer wept for the dogs, but now wept only for herself.

メルセデスはもう犬たちのことで泣かず、自分のことだけを思って泣いていた

She spent her time crying and quarreling with Hal and Charles.

彼女はハルとチャールズと泣きながら喧嘩して時間を過ごした

Quarreling was the one thing they were never too tired to do.

喧嘩だけは彼らにとって決して疲れることのない唯一のことだった

Their irritability came from misery, grew with it, and surpassed it.

彼らの怒りは悲惨さから生まれ、悲惨さとともに大きくなり、悲惨さを超えました

The patience of the trail, known to those who toil and suffer kindly, never came.

労苦を惜しまず親切に苦しむ人々に知られる道の忍耐は、決して訪れなかった

That patience, which keeps speech sweet through pain, was unknown to them.

苦痛の中でも言葉を優しく保つその忍耐力は彼らには知られていなかった

They had no hint of patience, no strength drawn from suffering with grace.

彼らには忍耐のかけらもなく、苦しみから恩恵を得て得られる強さもなかった

They were stiff with pain—aching in their muscles, bones, and hearts.

彼らは痛みで体が硬直し、筋肉、骨、心臓が痛みました

Because of this, they grew sharp of tongue and quick with harsh words.

このため、彼らは口が悪く、厳しい言葉をすぐに口にするようになった

Each day began and ended with angry voices and bitter complaints.

毎日は怒りの声と苦々しい不満で始まり、終わりました

Charles and Hal wrangled whenever Mercedes gave them a chance.

チャールズとハルは、メルセデスが機会を与えるたびに口論した

Each man believed he did more than his fair share of the work.

それぞれの男たちは、自分が与えられた仕事以上の成果をあげたと信じていた

Neither ever missed a chance to say so, again and again.

二人とも、何度も何度もそう言う機会を逃さなかった

Sometimes Mercedes sided with Charles, sometimes with Hal.

メルセデスは時々チャールズの味方をし、時々ハルの味方をしました

This led to a grand and endless quarrel among the three.
このことが、3人の間で壮大で終わりのない争いを引き起こした

A dispute over who should chop firewood grew out of control.
誰が薪を割るべきかという争いが制御不能になった

Soon, fathers, mothers, cousins, and dead relatives were named.
すぐに、父親、母親、いとこ、亡くなった親戚の名前が挙げられました

Hal's views on art or his uncle's plays became part of the fight.
ハルの芸術や叔父の演劇に対する見解が戦いの一部となった

Charles's political beliefs also entered the debate.
チャールズの政治的信念も議論に加わった

To Mercedes, even her husband's sister's gossip seemed relevant.
メルセデスにとっては、夫の妹の噂話さえも関係があるように思えた

She aired opinions on that and on many of Charles's family's flaws.
彼女はそのことやチャールズの家族の多くの欠点について意見を述べた

While they argued, the fire stayed unlit and camp half set.
彼らが言い争っている間にも火は消えたままで、キャンプの準備は半分整ったままだった

Meanwhile, the dogs remained cold and without any food.
その間、犬たちは寒さに震え、食べ物もありませんでした

Mercedes held a grievance she considered deeply personal.
メルセデスは、非常に個人的な恨みを抱いていた

She felt mistreated as a woman, denied her gentle privileges.
彼女は女性として不当な扱いを受け、優しい特権を否定されたと感じました

She was pretty and soft, and used to chivalry all her life.

彼女は可愛らしくて優しく、生涯を通じて騎士道精神を
貫きました

But her husband and brother now treated her with
impatience.

しかし、彼女の夫と兄は彼女を苛立たせる態度を取った

Her habit was to act helpless, and they began to complain.

彼女は無力なふりをするのが癖だったので、彼らは文句
を言い始めました

Offended by this, she made their lives all the more difficult.

彼女はこれに腹を立て、彼らの生活をさらに困難なもの
にした

She ignored the dogs and insisted on riding the sled herself.

彼女は犬を無視して自分でそりに乗ることを主張した

Though light in looks, she weighed one hundred twenty
pounds.

彼女は見た目は痩せ型だったが、体重は120ポンドあっ
た

That added burden was too much for the starving, weak
dogs.

その追加の負担は、飢えて弱っている犬たちにとっては
大きすぎました

Still, she rode for days, until the dogs collapsed in the reins.

それでも彼女は何日も馬に乗り続け、ついには犬たちが
手綱を握れなくなってしまった

The sled stood still, and Charles and Hal begged her to
walk.

そりは止まってしまい、チャールズとハルは彼女に歩い
て行くように頼みました

They pleaded and entreated, but she wept and called them
cruel.

彼らは嘆願し、懇願したが、彼女は泣きながら彼らを残
酷だと非難した

On one occasion, they pulled her off the sled with sheer
force and anger.

ある時、彼らは怒りと力で彼女をそりから引きずり落と
した

They never tried again after what happened that time.
彼らは、あの時の出来事以降、二度と試みることはなかった

She went limp like a spoiled child and sat in the snow.
彼女は甘やかされた子供のように力が抜けて雪の中に座った

They moved on, but she refused to rise or follow behind.
彼らは先に進みましたが、彼女は立ち上がることも、後を追うことも拒否しました

After three miles, they stopped, returned, and carried her back.
3マイル進んだところで彼らは立ち止まり、戻って彼女を抱きかかえて戻った

They reloaded her onto the sled, again using brute strength.
彼らは再び腕力を使って彼女をそりに乗せた

In their deep misery, they were callous to the dogs' suffering.
彼らは深い悲しみのあまり、犬たちの苦しみに無関心だった

Hal believed one must get hardened and forced that belief on others.
ハルは、人は心を強くしなければならないと信じ、その信念を他の人に押し付けました

He first tried to preach his philosophy to his sister
彼はまず妹に自分の哲学を説こうとした

and then, without success, he preached to his brother-in-law.
そして、彼は義理の兄弟に説教したが、効果はなかった

He had more success with the dogs, but only because he hurt them.
彼は犬に対してはより大きな成功を収めたが、それは彼が犬を傷つけたからに過ぎなかった

At Five Fingers, the dog food ran out of food completely.
ファイブ・フィンガーズでは、ドッグフードが完全になくなってしまいました

A toothless old squaw sold a few pounds of frozen horse-hide

歯のない老婆が数ポンドの凍った馬皮を売った

Hal traded his revolver for the dried horse-hide.

ハルはリボルバーを乾燥した馬の皮と交換した

The meat had come from starved horses of cattlemen months before.

その肉は数ヶ月前に牧場主の飢えた馬から採取されたものだった

Frozen, the hide was like galvanized iron; tough and inedible.

凍った皮は亜鉛メッキされた鉄のようになり、硬くて食べられませんでした

The dogs had to chew endlessly at the hide to eat it.

犬たちは皮を食べるために果てしなく噛み続けなければなりませんでした

But the leathery strings and short hair were hardly nourishment.

しかし、革のような紐と短い毛は、ほとんど栄養にはなりませんでした

Most of the hide was irritating, and not food in any true sense.

皮のほとんどは刺激が強く、本当の意味で食べ物ではありませんでした

And through it all, Buck staggered at the front, like in a nightmare.

そしてその間中、バックは悪夢の中のように先頭でよろめいていた

He pulled when able; when not, he lay until whip or club raised him.

彼はできるときは引っ張り、できないときは鞭か棍棒で起こされるまで横たわっていた

His fine, glossy coat had lost all stiffness and sheen it once had.

彼の上質で光沢のある毛皮は、かつての硬さと輝きをすっかり失っていました

His hair hung limp, draggled, and clotted with dried blood from the blows.

彼の髪はだらりと垂れ下がり、殴打による乾いた血で固まっていた

His muscles shrank to cords, and his flesh pads were all worn away.

彼の筋肉は縮んで紐のようになり、肉のパッドはすべてすり減っていました

Each rib, each bone showed clearly through folds of wrinkled skin.

しわくちゃの皮膚のひだを通して、肋骨の一本一本、骨の一本一本がはっきりと見えました

It was heartbreaking, yet Buck's heart could not break.

それは胸が張り裂けるような出来事だったが、バックの心は折れることはできなかった

The man in the red sweater had tested that and proved it long ago.

赤いセーターを着た男はずっと前にそれをテストして証明していました

As it was with Buck, so it was with all his remaining teammates.

バックの場合と同じように、残りのチームメイト全員も同様でした

There were seven in total, each one a walking skeleton of misery.

全部で 7 人がいて、それぞれが悲惨さの歩く骸骨でした

They had grown numb to lash, feeling only distant pain.

彼らは鞭打ちにも麻痺し、遠くの痛みしか感じなくなっていた

Even sight and sound reached them faintly, as through a thick fog.

濃い霧を通してのように、視覚や聴覚さえもかすかに彼らに届いた

They were not half alive—they were bones with dim sparks inside.

彼らは半分生きているわけではなく、内部にかすかな火花を散らしている骨だった

When stopped, they collapsed like corpses, their sparks almost gone.

止まると、彼らは死体のように崩れ落ち、火花はほとんど消えてしまいました

And when the whip or club struck again, the sparks fluttered weakly.

そして鞭か棍棒が再び打たれると、火花が弱々しく舞い上がった

Then they rose, staggered forward, and dragged their limbs ahead.

それから彼らは立ち上がり、よろめきながら前に進み、手足を引きずりながら前に進みました

One day kind Billee fell and could no longer rise at all.

ある日、優しいビリーは倒れてしまい、もう起き上がることができなくなってしまいました

Hal had traded his revolver, so he used an axe to kill Billee instead.

ハルはリボルバーを交換していたので、代わりに斧を使ってビリーを殺した

He struck him on the head, then cut his body free and dragged it away.

彼は男の頭を殴り、その体を切り離して引きずり出した

Buck saw this, and so did the others; they knew death was near.

バックはこれを見て、他の者たちもそれを見て、死が近いことを悟った

Next day Koona went, leaving just five dogs in the starving team.

翌日、クーナは出発し、飢えたチームには5匹の犬だけが残されました

Joe, no longer mean, was too far gone to be aware of much at all.

ジョーは、もう意地悪ではなかったが、あまりにもひどく気が狂っていて、ほとんど何も分かっていなかった

Pike, no longer faking his injury, was barely conscious.

パイクは、もはや怪我を偽ることはなく、ほとんど意識がなかった

Solleks, still faithful, mourned he had no strength to give.
ソレックスは依然忠実であり、与える力がないことを嘆いた

Teek was beaten most because he was fresher, but fading fast.
ティークは、より元気だったが急速に衰えていたため、最も打撃を受けた

And Buck, still in the lead, no longer kept order or enforced it.
そして、依然として先頭に立っていたバックは、もはや秩序を維持したり強制したりしなくなった

Half blind with weakness, Buck followed the trail by feel alone.
衰弱して半分目が見えなくなったバックは、感覚だけを頼りに道を追った

It was beautiful spring weather, but none of them noticed it.
美しい春の天気だったが、誰もそれに気づかなかった

Each day the sun rose earlier and set later than before.
毎日、太陽は以前よりも早く昇り、遅く沈むようになりました

By three in the morning, dawn had come; twilight lasted till nine.
午前3時までに夜明けが訪れ、夕暮れは9時まで続いた

The long days were filled with the full blaze of spring sunshine.
長い日々は、まばゆいばかりの春の太陽の光で満たされていた

The ghostly silence of winter had changed into a warm murmur.
冬の幽霊のような静寂は、暖かいささやきに変わっていた

All the land was waking, alive with the joy of living things.
全地は目覚め、生き物たちの喜びで活気づいていた

The sound came from what had lain dead and still through winter.

その音は、冬の間ずっと死んで動かなかったものから聞こえてきた

Now, those things moved again, shaking off the long frost sleep.

今、それらは長い凍てつく眠りから覚め、再び動き出した

Sap was rising through the dark trunks of the waiting pine trees.

待ち構える松の木々の暗い幹から樹液が上がってきていた

Willows and aspens burst out bright young buds on each twig.

柳やポプラの木々の枝一本一本に、輝くばかりの若芽が芽吹いた

Shrubs and vines put on fresh green as the woods came alive.

森が生き生きと動き出すにつれ、低木や蔓植物は新緑を帯びてきました

Crickets chirped at night, and bugs crawled in daylight sun.

夜にはコオロギが鳴き、昼間の太陽の下では虫が這っていました

Partridges boomed, and woodpeckers knocked deep in the trees.

ヤマウズラが鳴き声をあげ、キツツキが木の奥深くで鳴き声をあげた

Squirrels chattered, birds sang, and geese honked over the dogs.

リスがおしゃべりし、鳥が歌い、ガチョウが犬の上で鳴き声を上げていた

The wild-fowl came in sharp wedges, flying up from the south.

野鳥は鋭いくさび形の群れとなって南から飛んできた

From every hillside came the music of hidden, rushing streams.

どの丘の斜面からも、隠れた急流の音が聞こえてきました

All things thawed and snapped, bent and burst back into motion.

すべてのものは解けて折れ、曲がり、再び動き出した

The Yukon strained to break the cold chains of frozen ice.

ユーコンは凍った氷の冷たい鎖を断ち切ろうと努力した

The ice melted underneath, while the sun melted it from above.

氷は下から溶け、太陽は上から氷を溶かしました

Air-holes opened, cracks spread, and chunks fell into the river.

風穴が開き、亀裂が広がり、岩塊が川に落ちた

Amid all this bursting and blazing life, the travelers staggered.

この活気と輝きに満ちた生命の真っ只中で、旅人たちはよろめきながら歩いていた

Two men, a woman, and a pack of huskies walked like the dead.

2人の男、1人の女、そして一群のハスキー犬が死んだように歩いていた

The dogs were falling, Mercedes wept, but still rode the sled.

犬たちは倒れ、メルセデスは泣きながらも、そりに乗り続けた

Hal cursed weakly, and Charles blinked through watering eyes.

ハルは弱々しく悪態をつき、チャールズは涙目で瞬きした

They stumbled into John Thornton's camp by White River's mouth.

彼らはホワイト川の河口にあるジョン・ソーントンのキャンプに偶然たどり着いた

When they stopped, the dogs dropped flat, as if all struck dead.

彼らが立ち止まると、犬たちは全員死んだかのように平らに倒れた

Mercedes wiped her tears and looked across at John Thornton.

メルセデスは涙を拭ってジョン・ソーントンに視線を向けた

Charles sat on a log, slowly and stiffly, aching from the trail.

チャールズは、足跡の痛みを感じながら、ゆっくりと硬直した姿勢で丸太の上に座った

Hal did the talking as Thornton carved the end of an axe-handle.

ソーントンが斧の柄の端を彫っている間、ハルが話をしていた

He whittled birch wood and answered with brief, firm replies.

彼は樺の木を削りながら、短く、毅然とした返事を返した

When asked, he gave advice, certain it wasn't going to be followed.

尋ねられたとき、彼は、それが従われることはないだろうと確信しながらアドバイスをしました

Hal explained, "They told us the trail ice was dropping out."

ハルさんは「登山道の氷が溶けていると聞きました」と説明した

"They said we should stay put—but we made it to White River."

「彼らは私たちにそこに留まるように言ったが、私たちはホワイトリバーにたどり着いた」

He ended with a sneering tone, as if to claim victory in hardship.

彼は苦難に打ち勝ったかのように、冷笑的な口調で話を終えた

"And they told you true," John Thornton answered Hal quietly.

「そして彼らは本当のことを言ったんだ」ジョン・ソーントンは静かにハルに答えた

"The ice may give way at any moment—it's ready to drop out."

「氷はいつ崩れてもおかしくない、今にも崩れ落ちるかもしれない」

"Only blind luck and fools could have made it this far alive."

「ここまで生きて来られたのは、運と愚か者だけだった」

"I tell you straight, I wouldn't risk my life for all Alaska's gold."

「はっきり言いますが、私はアラスカの金のために命を危険にさらしたりはしません」

"That's because you're not a fool, I suppose," Hal answered.

「それはあなたが馬鹿ではないからだと思います」とハルは答えた

"All the same, we'll go on to Dawson." He uncoiled his whip.

「やはり、ドーソンへ行こう」彼は鞭を解いた

"Get up there, Buck! Hi! Get up! Go on!" he shouted harshly.

「あそこに立て、バック！おい！立て！行け！」彼は荒々しく叫んだ

Thornton kept whittling, knowing fools won't hear reason.

ソーントンは、愚か者は理屈を聞かないと分かっていながら、削り続けた

To stop a fool was futile—and two or three fooled changed nothing.

愚か者を止めるのは無駄だった二、三人が騙されても何も変わらなかった

But the team didn't move at the sound of Hal's command.

しかし、チームはハルの命令を聞いても動かなかった

By now, only blows could make them rise and pull forward.

今では、彼らを立ち上がらせ、前進させるには打撃を与えることしかできなかった

The whip snapped again and again across the weakened dogs.

鞭は弱った犬たちに何度も何度も打ち付けた

John Thornton pressed his lips tightly and watched in silence.

ジョン・ソーントンは唇を固く閉じて、黙って見守った

Solleks was the first to crawl to his feet under the lash.

鞭打ちの下で最初に這って立ち上がったのはソレックスだった

Then Teek followed, trembling. Joe yelped as he stumbled up.

ティークも震えながら後を追ってきたジョーはよろめきながら立ち上がり、悲鳴を上げた

Pike tried to rise, failed twice, then finally stood unsteadily.

パイクは立ち上がろうとしたが、二度失敗し、ついによろめきながら立ち上がった

But Buck lay where he had fallen, not moving at all this time.

しかし、バックは倒れた場所に横たわり、今度はまったく動かなかった

The whip slashed him over and over, but he made no sound.

鞭が何度も彼を打ったが、彼は音を立てなかった

He did not flinch or resist, simply remained still and quiet.

彼はひるむことも抵抗することもせず、ただじっと静かにしていた

Thornton stirred more than once, as if to speak, but didn't.

ソーントンは何かを言おうとするかのように何度も身じろぎしたが、何も言わなかった

His eyes grew wet, and still the whip cracked against Buck.

彼の目は潤んでいたが、鞭はまだバックに打ち付けられていた

At last, Thornton began pacing slowly, unsure of what to do.

ついに、ソーントンは何をすべきか分からず、ゆっくりと歩き始めた

It was the first time Buck had failed, and Hal grew furious.

バックが失敗したのは初めてだったので、ハルは激怒した

He threw down the whip and picked up the heavy club instead.

彼は鞭を投げ捨て、代わりに重い棍棒を手に取った

The wooden club came down hard, but Buck still did not rise to move.

木の棍棒が激しく振り下ろされたが、バックはまだ立ち上がって動かなかった

Like his teammates, he was too weak—but more than that.

チームメイトたちと同様、彼も弱すぎたしかし、それだけではなかった

Buck had decided not to move, no matter what came next.

バックは、次に何が起ころうとも動かないと決めていた

He felt something dark and certain hovering just ahead.

彼は、何か暗くて確かなものがすぐ前方に漂っているのを感じた

That dread had seized him as soon as he reached the riverbank.

その恐怖は彼が川岸に着くとすぐに彼を襲った

The feeling had not left him since he felt the ice thin under his paws.

足の下の氷が薄くなっているのを感じて以来、その感覚は消えていなかった

Something terrible was waiting—he felt it just down the trail.

何か恐ろしいものが待ち受けている ——
彼はそれをすぐ先の道で感じた

He wasn't going to walk towards that terrible thing ahead

彼はその恐ろしいものに向かって歩くつもりはなかった

He was not going to obey any command that took him to that thing.

彼は、自分をその場所に導くいかなる命令にも従うつもりはなかった

The pain of the blows hardly touched him now—he was too far gone.

打撃の痛みは、今では彼にはほとんど感じられなかった彼はすでに手遅れだったのだ

The spark of life flickered low, dimmed beneath each cruel strike.

生命の火花は、残酷な打撃を受けるたびに弱まり、消えていった

His limbs felt distant; his whole body seemed to belong to another.

彼の手足は遠く感じられ、彼の全身は他人のもののように思えた

He felt a strange numbness as the pain faded out completely.

痛みが完全に消え去ると、彼は奇妙なしびれを感じた

From far away, he sensed he was being beaten, but barely knew.

遠くから、彼は殴られているのを感じたが、ほとんど気づかなかった

He could hear the thuds faintly, but they no longer truly hurt.

かすかにドスンという音が聞こえたが、もう本当に痛いという感じではなかった

The blows landed, but his body no longer seemed like his own.

打撃は当たったが、彼の体はもはや自分の体とは思えなかった

Then suddenly, without warning, John Thornton gave a wild cry.

すると突然、何の前触れもなく、ジョン・ソーントンは激しい叫び声をあげた

It was inarticulate, more the cry of a beast than of a man.

それは不明瞭で、人間の叫びというよりは獣の叫びのようだった

He leapt at the man with the club and knocked Hal backward.

彼は棍棒を持って男に飛びかかり、ハルを後ろに押し倒した

Hal flew as if struck by a tree, landing hard upon the ground.

ハルはまるで木にぶつかったかのように飛び、地面に激しく着地した

Mercedes screamed aloud in panic and clutched at her face.
メルセデスはパニックになって大声で叫び、顔を押さえた

Charles only looked on, wiped his eyes, and stayed seated.
チャールズはただ見守り、目を拭いて、座ったままでした

His body was too stiff with pain to rise or help in the fight.
彼の体は痛みで硬直しており、立ち上がることも、戦いを手伝うこともできなかった

Thornton stood over Buck, trembling with fury, unable to speak.
ソーントンは怒りに震えながら、何も言えずにバックの上に立っていた

He shook with rage and fought to find his voice through it.
彼は怒りに震えながら、それを乗り越えて自分の声を見つけようと奮闘した

"If you strike that dog again, I'll kill you," he finally said.
「もう一度あの犬を殴ったら、お前を殺す」と彼はついに言った

Hal wiped blood from his mouth and came forward again.
ハルは口から血を拭って再び前に出た

"It's my dog," he muttered. "Get out of the way, or I'll fix you."
「俺の犬だ」と彼はぶつぶつ言った「どけ、さもないとお前を懲らしめるぞ」

"I'm going to Dawson, and you're not stopping me," he added.
「私はドーソンに行くつもりだあなたは私を止めることはできない」と彼は付け加えた

Thornton stood firm between Buck and the angry young man.
ソーントンはバックと怒った若者の間にしっかりと立ちはだかった

He had no intention of stepping aside or letting Hal pass.
彼は脇に退いたりハルを通したりするつもりはなかった

Hal pulled out his hunting knife, long and dangerous in hand.

ハルは長くて危険な狩猟用ナイフを取り出した

Mercedes screamed, then cried, then laughed in wild hysteria.

メルセデスは叫び、泣き、そして狂ったように笑いました

Thornton struck Hal's hand with his axe-handle, hard and fast.

ソーントンは斧の柄でハルの手を激しく素早く殴りつけた

The knife was knocked loose from Hal's grip and flew to the ground.

ナイフはハルの手から弾き落とされ、地面に落ちた

Hal tried to pick the knife up, and Thornton rapped his knuckles again.

ハルはナイフを拾おうとしたが、ソーントンは再び彼の指の関節を叩いた

Then Thornton stooped down, grabbed the knife, and held it.

それからソーントンはかがみ込んでナイフを掴み、それを握った

With two quick chops of the axe-handle, he cut Buck's reins.

彼は斧の柄を素早く二度振り下ろし、バックの手綱を切った

Hal had no fight left in him and stepped back from the dog.

ハルはもう戦う気力もなく、犬から後ずさりした

Besides, Mercedes needed both arms now to keep her upright.

その上、メルセデスは立ち上がるために両腕が必要だった

Buck was too near death to be of use for pulling a sled again.

バックは死に近かったので、再びそりを引くことはできなかった

A few minutes later, they pulled out, heading down the river.

数分後、彼らは船を出し、川下に向かっていった

Buck raised his head weakly and watched them leave the bank.
バックは弱々しく頭を上げて、彼らが岸から去っていくのを見守った

Pike led the team, with Solleks at the rear in the wheel spot.
パイクがチームをリードし、ソレックスが後方のステアリングを握った

Joe and Teek walked between, both limping with exhaustion.
ジョーとティークは二人とも疲れて足を引きずりながら、その間を歩いていった

Mercedes sat on the sled, and Hal gripped the long gee-pole.
メルセデスはそりに座り、ハルは長いジーポールを握った

Charles stumbled behind, his steps clumsy and uncertain.
チャールズはよろめきながら後ろを歩き、ぎこちなく不安な足取りだった

Thornton knelt by Buck and gently felt for broken bones.
ソーントンはバックのそばにひざまずき、骨折した骨がないか優しく触診した

His hands were rough but moved with kindness and care.
彼の手は荒れていたが、優しく気配りのある動きをしていた

Buck's body was bruised but showed no lasting injury.
バックの体は打撲傷を負っていたが、永続的な傷害は見られなかった

What remained was terrible hunger and near-total weakness.
残ったのはひどい飢えとほぼ完全な衰弱だけだった

By the time this was clear, the sled had gone far downriver.
それが明らかになったときには、そりは川のずっと下流へ進んでいました

Man and dog watched the sled slowly crawl over the cracking ice.
男と犬は、ひび割れた氷の上をそりがゆっくりと進んでいくのを見ていた

Then, they saw the sled sink down into a hollow.
すると、そりが窪みに沈んでいくのが見えました
The gee-pole flew up, with Hal still clinging to it in vain.
ジーポールは飛び上がり、ハルは無駄にそれにしがみついていた
Mercedes's scream reached them across the cold distance.
メルセデスの叫び声が冷たい距離を越えて彼らに届いた
Charles turned and stepped back—but he was too late.
チャールズは振り返って後ずさりしたが、遅すぎた
A whole ice sheet gave way, and they all dropped through.
氷床全体が崩れて、彼らは全員落ちてしまいました
Dogs, sled, and people vanished into the black water below.
犬、そり、そして人々は下の黒い水の中に消えていった
Only a wide hole in the ice was left where they had passed.
彼らが通った場所には、氷に大きな穴が残るだけだった
The trail's bottom had dropped out—just as Thornton warned.
道の底は抜け落ちていた ―
まさにソーントンが警告した通り
Thornton and Buck looked at one another, silent for a moment.
ソーントンとバックはお互いに顔を見合わせ、しばらく黙っていた
"You poor devil," said Thornton softly, and Buck licked his hand.
「かわいそうに」とソーントンは優しく言い、バックは彼の手を舐めた

For the Love of a Man
男の愛のために

John Thornton froze his feet in the cold of the previous December.
ジョン・ソーントンは前年の12月の寒さで足が凍えてしまった

His partners made him comfortable and left him to recover alone.
パートナーたちは彼を安心させて、一人で回復できるようにしてあげた

They went up the river to gather a raft of saw-logs for Dawson.
彼らはドーソンのために大量の丸太を集めるために川を上っていった

He was still limping slightly when he rescued Buck from death.
バックを死から救ったとき、彼はまだ少し足を引きずっていた

But with warm weather continuing, even that limp disappeared.
しかし、暖かい天気が続くと、足を引きずることもなくなりました

Lying by the riverbank during long spring days, Buck rested.
長い春の日々の間、バックは川岸に横たわり、休んだ

He watched the flowing water and listened to birds and insects.
彼は流れる水を眺め、鳥や昆虫の鳴き声に耳を傾けた

Slowly, Buck regained his strength under the sun and sky.
バックは太陽と空の下でゆっくりと体力を取り戻した

A rest felt wonderful after traveling three thousand miles.
3000マイルの旅の後、休息は素晴らしい気分でした

Buck became lazy as his wounds healed and his body filled out.

傷が治り、体が充実するにつれて、バックは怠惰になりました

His muscles grew firm, and flesh returned to cover his bones.

彼の筋肉は引き締まり、肉が戻って骨を覆うようになりました

They were all resting—Buck, Thornton, Skeet, and Nig.

バック、ソーントン、スキート、ニグは皆休んでいた

They waited for the raft that was going to carry them down to Dawson.

彼らはドーソンまで運んでくれるいかだを待った

Skeet was a small Irish setter who made friends with Buck.

スキートはバックと友達になった小さなアイリッシュ・セッターでした

Buck was too weak and ill to resist her at their first meeting.

バックは体調が悪すぎて、初めて彼女に会ったときには抵抗できなかった

Skeet had the healer trait that some dogs naturally possess.

スキートは、一部の犬が生まれつき持っている治癒能力を持っていました

Like a mother cat, she licked and cleaned Buck's raw wounds.

彼女は母猫のようにバックの生傷を舐めてきれいにしてあげました

Every morning after breakfast, she repeated her careful work.

彼女は毎朝朝食後に、念入りな仕事を繰り返した

Buck came to expect her help as much as he did Thornton's.

バックはソーントンの助けと同じくらい彼女の助けも期待するようになった

Nig was friendly too, but less open and less affectionate.

ニグも友好的でしたが、オープンさや愛情が足りませんでした

Nig was a big black dog, part bloodhound and part deerhound.

ニグは大きな黒い犬で、ブラッドハウンドとディアハウンドの混血種でした

He had laughing eyes and endless good nature in his spirit.
彼は笑っている目と、心の底に限りない善良さを持っていました

To Buck's surprise, neither dog showed jealousy toward him.
バックが驚いたことに、どちらの犬も彼に対して嫉妬を示さなかった

Both Skeet and Nig shared the kindness of John Thornton.
スキートとニグはともにジョン・ソーントンの親切にあずかりました

As Buck got stronger, they lured him into foolish dog games.
バックが強くなるにつれて、彼らは彼を愚かな犬のゲームに誘い込みました

Thornton often played with them too, unable to resist their joy.
ソーントンも彼らの喜びに抗うことができず、よく彼らと遊んでいました

In this playful way, Buck moved from illness to a new life.
この遊び心のあるやり方で、バックは病気から新しい人生へと移行しました

Love—true, burning, and passionate love—was his at last.
ついに彼の愛は真実の、燃えるような、情熱的な愛となった

He had never known this kind of love at Miller's estate.
彼はミラー邸でこのような愛を一度も知ったことはなかった

With the Judge's sons, he had shared work and adventure.
彼は判事の息子たちとともに仕事や冒険を共にした

With the grandsons, he saw stiff and boastful pride.
孫たちを見ると、堅苦しくて自慢げなプライドが感じられた

With Judge Miller himself, he had a respectful friendship.
彼はミラー判事自身と尊敬し合う友情を築いていた

But love that was fire, madness, and worship came with Thornton.

しかし、ソーントンには、情熱と狂気と崇拝に満ちた愛が宿っていた

This man had saved Buck's life, and that alone meant a great deal.

この男はバックの命を救ったそれだけでも大きな意味があった

But more than that, John Thornton was the ideal kind of master.

しかし、それ以上に、ジョン・ソーントンは理想的なマスターでした

Other men cared for dogs out of duty or business necessity.

他の男性は義務や業務上の必要性から犬の世話をしました

John Thornton cared for his dogs as if they were his children.

ジョン・ソーントンは犬たちをまるで自分の子供のように大切にしていた

He cared for them because he loved them and simply could not help it.

彼は彼らを愛していたので、彼らを気遣うしかなかったのです

John Thornton saw even further than most men ever managed to see.

ジョン・ソーントンは、ほとんどの人が見ることができなかったほど遠くまで見通すことができました

He never forgot to greet them kindly or speak a cheering word.

彼は彼らに優しく挨拶したり励ましの言葉をかけたりすることを決して忘れなかった

He loved sitting down with the dogs for long talks, or "gassy," as he said.

彼は犬たちと一緒に座って長い話をするのが大好きで、彼の言葉を借りれば「ガスっぽい」会話をするのが大好きだった

He liked to seize Buck's head roughly between his strong hands.

彼は力強い手でバックの頭を乱暴に掴むのが好きだった

Then he rested his own head against Buck's and shook him gently.

それから彼は自分の頭をバックの頭に寄りかからせ、優しく頭を揺すった

All the while, he called Buck rude names that meant love to Buck.

その間ずっと、彼はバックに対して、愛を意味する失礼な言葉を浴びせ続けた

To Buck, that rough embrace and those words brought deep joy.

バックにとって、その荒々しい抱擁と言葉は深い喜びをもたらした

His heart seemed to shake loose with happiness at each movement.

彼の心は動くたびに幸せで震え上がるようだった

When he sprang up afterward, his mouth looked like it laughed.

その後、彼が飛び上がったとき、彼の口は笑っているように見えました

His eyes shone brightly and his throat trembled with unspoken joy.

彼の目は明るく輝き、喉は言葉にできない喜びで震えていた

His smile stood still in that state of emotion and glowing affection.

彼の笑顔は、その感動と熱烈な愛情の状態で静止していた

Then Thornton exclaimed thoughtfully, "God! he can almost speak!"

するとソーントンは考え深げに叫んだ「なんてことだ！彼はほとんど話せるようだ！」

Buck had a strange way of expressing love that nearly caused pain.

バックは、ほとんど痛みを引き起こすような奇妙な愛情表現をしていた

He often griped Thornton's hand in his teeth very tightly.

彼はよくソーントンの手を歯で強く握りしめていた

The bite was going to leave deep marks that stayed for some time after.

その噛み跡は、しばらく残る深い跡を残すことになるだろう

Buck believed those oaths were love, and Thornton knew the same.

バックはそれらの誓いが愛だと信じていたし、ソーントンも同じことを知っていた

Most often, Buck's love showed in quiet, almost silent adoration.

ほとんどの場合、バックの愛は静かでほとんど沈黙した崇拝の形で表れていた

Though thrilled when touched or spoken to, he did not seek attention.

触られたり話しかけられたりすると興奮しましたが、注目を求めませんでした

Skeet nudged her nose under Thornton's hand until he petted her.

スキートはソーントンの手の下で鼻を軽くつつき、ソーントンは彼女を撫でた

Nig walked up quietly and rested his large head on Thornton's knee.

ニグは静かに歩み寄り、大きな頭をソーントンの膝の上に置いた

Buck, in contrast, was satisfied to love from a respectful distance.

対照的に、バックは敬意を持った距離から愛することで満足していた

He lied for hours at Thornton's feet, alert and watching closely.

彼はソーントンの足元に何時間も横たわり、油断せずに注意深く見守っていた

Buck studied every detail of his master's face and slightest motion.

バックは主人の顔の表情やわずかな動きを細部まで観察した

Or lied farther away, studying the man's shape in silence.

あるいは、さらに離れたところに横たわり、黙って男の姿を観察していた

Buck watched each small move, each shift in posture or gesture.

バックは、あらゆる小さな動き、姿勢や身振りの変化を観察した

So powerful was this connection that often pulled Thornton's gaze.

このつながりは非常に強力で、ソーントンはしばしば視線を惹きつけました

He met Buck's eyes with no words, love shining clearly through.

彼は言葉もなくバックの目を見つめたが、そこには明らかに愛が輝いていた

For a long while after being saved, Buck never let Thornton out of sight.

救出された後も長い間、バックはソーントンから目を離さなかった

Whenever Thornton left the tent, Buck followed him closely outside.

ソーントンがテントから出かけると、バックはいつもすぐ後をついて出て行った

All the harsh masters in the Northland had made Buck afraid to trust.

北国の厳しい主人たちのせいで、バックは信頼することを恐れていた

He feared no man could remain his master for more than a short time.

彼は、誰も短期間以上は自分の主人であり続けることはできないだろうと恐れていた

He feared John Thornton was going to vanish like Perrault and François.

彼はジョン・ソーントンがペローやフランソワのように消えてしまうのではないかと恐れていた

Even at night, the fear of losing him haunted Buck's restless sleep.

夜になっても、彼を失うかもしれないという恐怖がバックの眠れない眠りを悩ませた

When Buck woke, he crept out into the cold, and went to the tent.

バックは目を覚ますと、寒い外に忍び出てテントへ向かった

He listened carefully for the soft sound of breathing inside.

彼は内部のかすかな呼吸の音を注意深く聞き取った

Despite Buck's deep love for John Thornton, the wild stayed alive.

バックがジョン・ソーントンを深く愛していたにもかかわらず、野生は生き残った

That primitive instinct, awakened in the North, did not disappear.

北で目覚めたその原始的な本能は消えなかった

Love brought devotion, loyalty, and the fire-side's warm bond.

愛は献身、忠誠、そして暖炉のそばでの温かい絆をもたらしました

But Buck also kept his wild instincts, sharp and ever alert.

しかし、バックは野生の本能も持ち続け、鋭敏で常に警戒していました

He was not just a tamed pet from the soft lands of civilization.

彼は、単に文明の穏やかな土地から来た飼い慣らされたペットではありませんでした

Buck was a wild being who had come in to sit by Thornton's fire.

バックはソーントンの火のそばに座りに来た野生の生き物だった

He looked like a Southland dog, but wildness lived within him.

彼はサウスランドの犬のように見えたが、彼の中には野性が宿っていた

His love for Thornton was too great to allow theft from the man.

ソーントンに対する彼の愛はあまりにも深かったので、彼から盗むことは許せなかった

But in any other camp, he would steal boldly and without pause.

しかし、他のキャンプであれば、彼はためらうことなく大胆に盗みを働くだろう

He was so clever in stealing that no one could catch or accuse him.

彼は盗みがとても巧妙だったので、誰も彼を捕まえたり告発したりすることはできなかった

His face and body were covered in scars from many past fights.

彼の顔と体は過去の数々の戦いによる傷跡で覆われていた

Buck still fought fiercely, but now he fought with more cunning.

バックは相変わらず激しく戦ったが、今度はもっと狡猾に戦った

Skeet and Nig were too gentle to fight, and they were Thornton's.

スキートとニグは戦うにはあまりにも穏やかで、彼らはソーントンの犬でした

But any strange dog, no matter how strong or brave, gave way.

しかし、どんなに強くて勇敢な犬でも、見知らぬ犬は道を譲りました

Otherwise, the dog found itself battling Buck; fighting for its life.

そうでなければ、犬はバックと闘い、自分の命をかけて戦うことになるだろう

Buck had no mercy once he chose to fight against another dog.

バックは、他の犬と戦うことを選んだら容赦しませんでした

He had learned well the law of club and fang in the Northland.

彼は北国の棍棒と牙の法則をよく学んでいた

He never gave up an advantage and never backed away from battle.

彼は決して優位性を放棄せず、戦いから逃げることもなかった

He had studied Spitz and the fiercest dogs of mail and police.

彼はスピッツと郵便や警察の最も獰猛な犬を研究した

He knew clearly there was no middle ground in wild combat.

彼は激しい戦闘には中立の立場など存在しないことを明らかに知っていた

He must rule or be ruled; showing mercy meant showing weakness.

彼は支配するか、支配されるかのどちらかであり、慈悲を示すことは弱さを示すことを意味した

Mercy was unknown in the raw and brutal world of survival.

生き残るための荒々しく残酷な世界では慈悲は知られていなかった

To show mercy was seen as fear, and fear led quickly to death.

慈悲を示すことは恐怖と見なされ、恐怖はすぐに死につながりました

The old law was simple: kill or be killed, eat or be eaten.

昔の法律は単純だった殺すか殺されるか、食べるか食べられるか

That law came from the depths of time, and Buck followed it fully.

その法則は時の深淵から生まれたものであり、バックはそれを完全に従った

Buck was older than his years and the number of breaths he took.

バックは、年齢や呼吸の数よりも老けて見えた

He connected the ancient past with the present moment clearly.

彼は古代の過去と現在の瞬間を明確に結びつけた

The deep rhythms of the ages moved through him like the tides.

時代の深いリズムが潮のように彼の中に流れていった

Time pulsed in his blood as surely as seasons moved the earth.

季節が地球を動かすのと同じように、時間は彼の血の中で確実に脈打っていた

He sat by Thornton's fire, strong-chested and white-fanged.

彼は胸が強く、牙が白く、ソーントンの暖炉のそばに座っていた

His long fur waved, but behind him the spirits of wild dogs watched.

長い毛が揺れていたが、その背後では野犬の霊が見守っていた

Half-wolves and full wolves stirred within his heart and senses.

半狼と全狼が彼の心と感覚の中で動いた

They tasted his meat and drank the same water that he did.

彼らは彼の肉を味わい、彼と同じ水を飲みました

They sniffed the wind alongside him and listened to the forest.

彼らは彼と一緒に風を嗅ぎ、森の音に耳を傾けました

They whispered the meanings of the wild sounds in the darkness.

彼らは暗闇の中で荒々しい音の意味をささやいた

They shaped his moods and guided each of his quiet reactions.

それらは彼の気分を形作り、彼の静かな反応のそれぞれを導きました

They lay with him as he slept and became part of his deep dreams.

彼らは彼が眠っている間、彼と一緒に横たわり、彼の深い夢の一部となった

They dreamed with him, beyond him, and made up his very spirit.

彼らは彼とともに、彼を超えて夢を見て、彼の精神そのものを作り上げました

The spirits of the wild called so strongly that Buck felt pulled.

野生の精霊の呼びかけがあまりにも強かったので、バックは引っ張られるのを感じた

Each day, mankind and its claims grew weaker in Buck's heart.

人類とその主張は、バックの心の中で日に日に弱まっていった

Deep in the forest, a strange and thrilling call was going to rise.

森の奥深くで、奇妙でスリリングな声が響き渡ろうとしていた

Every time he heard the call, Buck felt an urge he could not resist.

その呼び声を聞くたびに、バックは抵抗できない衝動を感じた

He was going to turn from the fire and from the beaten human paths.

彼は火と踏みならされた人間の道から離れようとしていた

He was going to plunge into the forest, going forward without knowing why.

彼は理由も分からず、森の中へと突き進んでいくつもりだった

He did not question this pull, for the call was deep and powerful.

彼はこの引力に疑問を持たなかったその呼び声は深く、強力だったからだ

Often, he reached the green shade and soft untouched earth
彼はしばしば緑の陰と柔らかい手つかずの土に辿り着いた

But then the strong love for John Thornton pulled him back to the fire.
しかし、ジョン・ソーントンへの強い愛情が彼を再び火の中に引き戻したのです

Only John Thornton truly held Buck's wild heart in his grasp.
ジョン・ソーントンだけが、バックの荒々しい心を本当に掴んでいた

The rest of mankind had no lasting value or meaning to Buck.
残りの人類にはバックにとって永続的な価値も意味もなかった

Strangers might praise him or stroke his fur with friendly hands.
見知らぬ人が彼を褒めたり、友好的な手で彼の毛を撫でたりするかもしれません

Buck remained unmoved and walked off from too much affection.
バックは、あまりの愛情に動じることなく立ち去った

Hans and Pete arrived with the raft that had long been awaited
ハンスとピートは待ちに待ったいかだを持って到着した

Buck ignored them until he learned they were close to Thornton.
バックは彼らがソーントンの近くにいることを知るまで彼らを無視した

After that, he tolerated them, but never showed them full warmth.
その後、彼は彼らを容認はしたものの、彼らに全面的な温かさを見せることはなかった

He took food or kindness from them as if doing them a favor.

彼はまるで彼らに親切にするかのように、彼らから食べ物や親切を受け取りました

They were like Thornton—simple, honest, and clear in thought.

彼らはソーントンのように単純で、正直で、考えが明晰でした

All together they traveled to Dawson's saw-mill and the great eddy

彼らは全員一緒にドーソンの製材所とグレートエディへ旅した

On their journey the learned to understand Buck's nature deeply.

旅の途中で彼らはバックの本質を深く理解するようになった

They did not try to grow close like Skeet and Nig had done.

彼らはスキートとニグのように親しくなろうとはしなかった

But Buck's love for John Thornton only deepened over time.

しかし、バックのジョン・ソーントンに対する愛情は時とともに深まるばかりだった

Only Thornton could place a pack on Buck's back in the summer.

夏にバックの背中にパックを載せることができたのはソーントンだけだった

Whatever Thornton commanded, Buck was willing to do fully.

ソーントンが命じたことは何でも、バックは喜んで全力で従った

One day, after they left Dawson for the headwaters of the Tanana,

ある日、ドーソンを出発してタナナ川の源流に向かったとき、

the group sat on a cliff that dropped three feet to bare bedrock.

グループは、岩盤がむき出しになるまで3フィート下がった崖の上に座っていた

John Thornton sat near the edge, and Buck rested beside him.

ジョン・ソーントンは端の近くに座り、バックはその隣で休んだ

Thornton had a sudden thought and called the men's attention.

ソーントンは突然思いついて、男たちの注意を促した

He pointed across the chasm and gave Buck a single command.

彼は峡谷の向こうを指差してバックに一つの命令を下した

"Jump, Buck!" he said, swinging his arm out over the drop.

「ジャンプ、バック！」彼は腕を振り上げて落下地点を超えた

In a moment, he had to grab Buck, who was leaping to obey.

すぐに、彼は、従うために飛び上がっていたバックをつかまなければなりませんでした

Hans and Pete rushed forward and pulled both back to safety.

ハンスとピートは急いで前に進み出て、二人を安全な場所まで引き戻しました

After all ended, and they had caught their breath, Pete spoke up.

すべてが終わり、彼らが息を整えた後、ピートが口を開いた

"The love's uncanny," he said, shaken by the dog's fierce devotion.

「その愛は不思議なものだ」と彼は犬の激しい献身に心を揺さぶられながら言った

Thornton shook his head and replied with calm seriousness.

ソーントンは首を横に振り、冷静に真剣な表情で答えた

"No, the love is splendid," he said, "but also terrible."

「いや、愛は素晴らしい」と彼は言った「しかしまた恐ろしいものでもある」

"Sometimes, I must admit, this kind of love makes me afraid."

「時々、この種の愛は私を怖がらせると認めざるを得ません」

Pete nodded and said, "I'd hate to be the man who touches you."

ピートはうなずいて言った「君に触れる男にはなりたくないな」

He looked at Buck as he spoke, serious and full of respect.

彼は話しながら、真剣な表情と敬意を込めてバックを見つめた

"Py Jingo!" said Hans quickly. "Me either, no sir."

「ピィ・ジンゴ！」ハンスは慌てて言った「僕もです、旦那様」

Before the year ended, Pete's fears came true at Circle City.

その年が終わる前に、ピートの恐れはサークル・シティで現実になった

A cruel man named Black Burton picked a fight in the bar.

ブラック・バートンという名の冷酷な男がバーで喧嘩を売ってきた

He was angry and malicious, lashing out at a new tenderfoot.

彼は怒りと悪意に満ち、新しく入社したばかりの者を激しく攻撃した

John Thornton stepped in, calm and good-natured as always.

ジョン・ソーントンがいつものように落ち着いて温厚な態度で介入した

Buck lay in a corner, head down, watching Thornton closely.

バックは頭を下げて隅に横たわり、ソーントンをじっと見つめていた

Burton suddenly struck, his punch sending Thornton spinning.

バートンが突然攻撃を仕掛け、そのパンチでソーントンは回転した

Only the bar's rail kept him from crashing hard to the ground.
バーのレールだけが、彼が地面に激しく衝突するのを防いでいた
The watchers heard a sound that was not bark or yelp
監視員たちは吠え声でも鳴き声でもない音を聞いた
a deep roar came from Buck as he launched toward the man.
バックが男に向かって突進すると、低い叫び声が上がった
Burton threw his arm up and barely saved his own life.
バートンは腕を上げて、かろうじて自分の命を救った
Buck crashed into him, knocking him flat onto the floor.
バックは彼に激突し、彼を床に叩きつけた
Buck bit deep into the man's arm, then lunged for the throat.
バックは男の腕を深く噛み、それから喉に突進した
Burton could only partly block, and his neck was torn open.
バートンは部分的にしかブロックできず、首が裂けてしまった
Men rushed in, clubs raised, and drove Buck off the bleeding man.
男たちが突入し、棍棒を振り上げ、血を流している男のバックを追い払った
A surgeon worked quickly to stop the blood from flowing out.
外科医はすぐに血の流出を止める手術を行った
Buck paced and growled, trying to attack again and again.
雄鹿は歩き回り、うなり声をあげ、何度も攻撃しようとした
Only swinging clubs kept him back from reaching Burton.
スイングクラブだけが彼をバートンに近づけないようにしていた
A miners' meeting was called and held right there on the spot.
炭鉱労働者の集会が招集され、その場で開催されました
They agreed Buck had been provoked and voted to set him free.

彼らはバックが挑発されたことに同意し、彼を釈放する
ことに投票した

But Buck's fierce name now echoed in every camp in Alaska.
しかし、バックの勇ましい名前は、今やアラスカのあら
ゆるキャンプに響き渡っていた

Later that fall, Buck saved Thornton again in a new way.
その年の秋、バックは新たな方法で再びソーントンを救
った

The three men were guiding a long boat down rough rapids.
３人の男は長いボートを操縦して、激しい急流を下って
いた

Thornton maned the boat, calling directions to the shoreline.
ソーントンはボートを操縦し、岸までの道順を指示した

Hans and Pete ran on land, holding a rope from tree to tree.
ハンスとピートは木から木へとロープをつかみながら陸
上を走りました

Buck kept pace on the bank, always watching his master.
バックは主人を常に見守りながら、岸辺を歩き続けた

At one nasty place, rocks jutted out under the fast water.
ある厄介な場所では、速い水の下に岩が突き出ていまし
た

Hans let go of the rope, and Thornton steered the boat wide.
ハンスはロープを放し、ソーントンはボートを大きく舵
取りした

Hans sprinted to catch the boat again past the dangerous
rocks.
ハンスは危険な岩を通り過ぎて再びボートに追いつくた
めに全力疾走した

The boat cleared the ledge but hit a stronger part of the
current.
ボートは岩棚を越えたが、流れのより強い部分にぶつか
った

Hans grabbed the rope too quickly and pulled the boat off
balance.
ハンスはロープを素早く掴みすぎたため、ボートのバラ
ンスを崩してしまいました

The boat flipped over and slammed into the bank, bottom up.

ボートはひっくり返って底を上にして岸に激突した

Thornton was thrown out and swept into the wildest part of the water.

ソーントンは投げ出され、水の最も荒れた部分へと流された

No swimmer could have survived in those deadly, racing waters.

あの危険な流れの激しい水の中では、どんな水泳選手も生き残れなかっただろう

Buck jumped in instantly and chased his master down the river.

バックはすぐに飛び込んで、主人を川下まで追いかけました

After three hundred yards, he reached Thornton at last.

300ヤードを歩いて、ついに彼はソーントンに到着した

Thornton grabbed Buck's tail, and Buck turned for the shore.

ソーントンはバックの尻尾をつかみ、バックは岸の方へ向きを変えた

He swam with full strength, fighting the water's wild drag.

彼は水の激しい抵抗と戦いながら全力で泳いだ

They moved downstream faster than they could reach the shore.

彼らは岸に着くよりも速く下流へ移動した

Ahead, the river roared louder as it fell into deadly rapids.

前方では、川がさらに大きな轟音を立てて、致命的な急流に落ちていった

Rocks sliced through the water like the teeth of a huge comb.

岩が巨大な櫛の歯のように水を切り裂いた

The pull of the water near the drop was savage and inescapable.

滝の近くの水の引力は猛烈で逃れられないものでした

Thornton knew they could never make the shore in time.

ソーントンは彼らが時間通りに岸に着くことは絶対に不可能だと知っていた

He scraped over one rock, smashed across a second,
彼は一つの岩を擦り、もう一つの岩を叩き、

And then he crashed into a third rock, grabbing it with both hands.
そして彼は3つ目の岩にぶつかり、両手でそれを掴みました

He let go of Buck and shouted over the roar, "Go, Buck! Go!"
彼はバックを放し、轟音の中で叫びました「行け、バック！行け！」

Buck could not stay afloat and was swept down by the current.
バックは浮かんでいられず、流れに流されてしまった

He fought hard, struggling to turn, but made no headway at all.
彼は一生懸命抵抗し、方向転換しようとしたが、まったく前進しなかった

Then he heard Thornton repeat the command over the river's roar.
すると、ソーントンが川の轟音にかき消されずに命令を繰り返す声が聞こえた

Buck reared out of the water, raised his head as if for a last look.
バックは水から立ち上がって、最後にもう一度見ようとするかのように頭を上げた

then turned and obeyed, swimming toward the bank with resolve.
それから向きを変えて従い、決意を持って岸に向かって泳ぎました

Pete and Hans pulled him ashore at the final possible moment.
ピートとハンスは最後の瞬間に彼を岸に引き上げた

They knew Thornton could cling to the rock for only minutes more.

彼らは、ソーントンがあと数分しか岩にしがみついてい
られないことを知っていた

They ran up the bank to a spot far above where he was
hanging.

彼らは土手を駆け上がり、彼がぶら下がっている場所よ
りずっと上の地点まで行った

They tied the boat's line to Buck's neck and shoulders
carefully.

彼らはボートのロープをバックの首と肩に慎重に結び付
けた

The rope was snug but loose enough for breathing and
movement.

ロープはぴったりとフィットしていましたが、呼吸や動
きに支障のない程度に緩んでいました

Then they launched him into the rushing, deadly river
again.

それから彼らは彼を再び激流の危険な川に投げ込んだ

Buck swam boldly but missed his angle into the stream's
force.

バックは大胆に泳いだが、流れの勢いに逆らって泳ぐ角
度を間違えた

He saw too late that he was going to drift past Thornton.

彼はソーントンを通り過ぎようとしていることに気づく
のが遅すぎた

Hans jerked the rope tight, as if Buck were a capsizing boat.

ハンスは、まるでバックが転覆する船であるかのように
、ロープを強く引っ張った

The current pulled him under, and he vanished below the
surface.

彼は流れに引き込まれ、水面下に消えていった

His body struck the bank before Hans and Pete pulled him
out.

ハンスとピートが彼を引き上げる前に、彼の体は岸に激
突した

He was half-drowned, and they pounded the water out of
him.

彼は半分溺れていたが、彼らは彼から水を叩き出した
Buck stood, staggered, and collapsed again onto the ground.
バックは立ち上がり、よろめき、再び地面に倒れた
Then they heard Thornton's voice faintly carried by the wind.
そのとき、彼らは風に乗ってかすかにソーントンの声が聞こえた
Though the words were unclear, they knew he was near death.
言葉は不明瞭だったが、彼らは彼が死期が近いことを知った
The sound of Thornton's voice hit Buck like an electric jolt.
ソーントンの声がバックに電撃のように衝撃を与えた
He jumped up and ran up the bank, returning to the launch point.
彼は飛び上がって土手を駆け上がり、出発地点に戻った
Again they tied the rope to Buck, and again he entered the stream.
再び彼らはバックにロープを結び、バックは再び川に入った
This time, he swam directly and firmly into the rushing water.
今度は、彼は勢いよく流れ込む水の中へまっすぐに、そしてしっかりと泳ぎ込んだ
Hans let out the rope steadily while Pete kept it from tangling.
ハンスはロープを着実に繰り出し、ピートはロープが絡まらないようにした
Buck swam hard until he was lined up just above Thornton.
バックはソーントンの真上に並ぶまで懸命に泳ぎ続けた
Then he turned and charged down like a train in full speed.
それから彼は向きを変え、全速力で走る列車のように突進しました
Thornton saw him coming, braced, and locked arms around his neck.

ソーントンは彼が近づいてくるのを見て、身構え、彼の首に腕を回した

Hans tied the rope fast around a tree as both were pulled under.

ハンスは二人が引き込まれると、ロープを木の周りにしっかりと結びました

They tumbled underwater, smashing into rocks and river debris.

彼らは水中に転落し、岩や川の残骸に激突した

One moment Buck was on top, the next Thornton rose gasping.

一瞬バックが優位に立ったが、次の瞬間ソーントンが息を切らしながら立ち上がった

Battered and choking, they veered to the bank and safety.

打ちのめされ、窒息しそうになりながら、彼らは岸へと転進し安全な場所に避難した

Thornton regained consciousness, lying across a drift log.

ソーントンは流木の上に横たわり、意識を取り戻した

Hans and Pete worked him hard to bring back breath and life.

ハンスとピートは彼に呼吸と命を取り戻すために懸命に働きました

His first thought was for Buck, who lay motionless and limp.

彼の最初の考えは、動かずぐったりと横たわっているバックのことだった

Nig howled over Buck's body, and Skeet licked his face gently.

ニグはバックの体の上で吠え、スキートはバックの顔を優しく舐めた

Thornton, sore and bruised, examined Buck with careful hands.

ソーントンは、痛みと傷を負いながらも、慎重にバックを診察した

He found three ribs broken, but no deadly wounds in the dog.

犬の肋骨が3本折れているのが見つかったが、致命傷はなかった

"That settles it," Thornton said. "We camp here." And they did.

「それで決まりだ」とソーントンは言った「ここでキャンプする」そして彼らは実際にキャンプした

They stayed until Buck's ribs healed and he could walk again.

彼らはバックの肋骨が治り、彼が再び歩けるようになるまでそこに留まりました

That winter, Buck performed a feat that raised his fame further.

その冬、バックは彼の名声をさらに高める偉業を成し遂げた

It was less heroic than saving Thornton, but just as impressive.

それはソーントンを救ったことほど英雄的ではなかったが、同じくらい印象的だった

At Dawson, the partners needed supplies for a distant journey.

ドーソンでは、パートナーたちは遠出の旅に必要な物資を必要としていました

They wanted to travel East, into untouched wilderness lands.

彼らは東の、人の手が入っていない荒野へ旅したいと考えていました

Buck's deed in the Eldorado Saloon made that trip possible.

エルドラド・サルーンでのバックの功績により、その旅が可能になった

It began with men bragging about their dogs over drinks.

それは、酒を飲みながら自分の犬を自慢する男性たちから始まった

Buck's fame made him the target of challenges and doubt.

バックの名声のせいで、彼は挑戦と疑いの的となった

Thornton, proud and calm, stood firm in defending Buck's name.

ソーントンは誇り高く冷静に、バックの名誉を守るために毅然とした態度を貫いた

One man said his dog could pull five hundred pounds with ease.

ある男性は、自分の犬は500ポンドを楽々と引っ張ることができると言いました

Another said six hundred, and a third bragged seven hundred.

別の者は600だと言い、3人目は700だと自慢した

"Pfft!" said John Thornton, "Buck can pull a thousand pound sled."

「ふん！」ジョン・ソーントンは言った「バックは1000ポンドのそりを引けるんだぞ」

Matthewson, a Bonanza King, leaned forward and challenged him.

ボナンザ・キングのマシューソンは身を乗り出して彼に挑戦した

"You think he can put that much weight into motion?"

「彼はそんなに重いものを動かせると思いますか？」

"And you think he can pull the weight a full hundred yards?"

「それで、彼は100ヤードも重量物を引っ張れると思いますか？」

Thornton replied coolly, "Yes. Buck is dog enough to do it."

ソーントンは冷静に答えた「ああバックはそれをやるだけの力がある」

"He'll put a thousand pounds into motion, and pull it a hundred yards."

「彼は1000ポンドを動かして、それを100ヤード引っ張るでしょう」

Matthewson smiled slowly and made sure all men heard his words.

マシューソンはゆっくりと微笑み、全員が自分の言葉を聞いていることを確認した

"I've got a thousand dollars that says he can't. There it is."
「彼には無理だと証明する1000ドルの証拠があるこれだ」

He slammed a sack of gold dust the size of sausage on the bar.
彼はソーセージほどの大きさの金粉の袋をバーに叩きつけた

Nobody said a word. The silence grew heavy and tense around them.
誰も一言も発しなかった周囲に重苦しい沈黙と緊張が漂った

Thornton's bluff—if it was one—had been taken seriously.
ソーントンのブラフは、もしそうであったとしても、真剣に受け止められた

He felt heat rise in his face as blood rushed to his cheeks.
彼は頬に血が上って顔が熱くなるのを感じた

His tongue had gotten ahead of his reason in that moment.
その瞬間、彼の言葉は理性を先取りしていた

He truly didn't know if Buck could move a thousand pounds.
バックが1000ポンドを動かせるかどうか、彼には本当にわからなかった

Half a ton! The size of it alone made his heart feel heavy.
なんと半トン！その大きさだけでも胸が重くなる

He had faith in Buck's strength and had thought him capable.
彼はバックの強さを信頼しており、彼が有能だと考えていた

But he had never faced this kind of challenge, not like this.
しかし、彼はこのような種類の課題に直面したことがなかった

A dozen men watched him quietly, waiting to see what he'd do.
12人の男たちが静かに彼を見て、彼が何をするかを待っていた

He didn't have the money—neither did Hans or Pete.

彼にはお金がなかったハンスにもピートにもお金がなかった

"I've got a sled outside," said Matthewson coldly and direct.
「外にそりがあるよ」とマシューソンは冷たく直接言った

"It's loaded with twenty sacks, fifty pounds each, all flour.
「20袋、それぞれ50ポンドの小麦粉が詰まっています

So don't let a missing sled be your excuse now," he added.
だから今は、そりがなくなったことを言い訳にしてはいけない」と彼は付け加えた

Thornton stood silent. He didn't know what words to offer.
ソーントンは黙って立っていた何と言えばいいのか分からなかった

He looked around at the faces without seeing them clearly.
彼ははっきりと顔は見えないまま、周囲を見回した

He looked like a man frozen in thought, trying to restart.
彼は、考え込んで立ち直ろうとしている男のように見えた

Then he saw Jim O'Brien, a friend from the Mastodon days.
すると彼は、マストドン時代の友人であるジム・オブライエンに会った

That familiar face gave him courage he didn't know he had.
その馴染みのある顔は、彼に、自分が持っているとは知らなかった勇気を与えた

He turned and asked in a low voice, "Can you lend me a thousand?"
彼は振り返って低い声で尋ねました「1000ドル貸してもらえますか?」

"Sure," said O'Brien, dropping a heavy sack by the gold already.
「もちろんだ」オブライエンは、重い袋を金貨のそばに落としながら言った

"But truthfully, John, I don't believe the beast can do this."
「でも正直に言うと、ジョン、あの獣がそんなことできるとは思えないよ」

Everyone in the Eldorado Saloon rushed outside to see the event.

エルドラド・サルーンにいた全員が、その出来事を見るために外に駆け出しました

They left tables and drinks, and even the games were paused.

彼らはテーブルと飲み物を去り、ゲームさえも中断しました

Dealers and gamblers came to witness the bold wager's end.

ディーラーとギャンブラーたちは、大胆な賭けの結末を見届けるためにやって来た

Hundreds gathered around the sled in the icy open street.

凍った広い道路に置かれたそりの周りには何百人もの人が集まりました

Matthewson's sled stood with a full load of flour sacks.

マシューソンのそりには小麦粉の袋が満載されていた

The sled had been sitting for hours in minus temperatures.

そりはマイナス気温の中で何時間も放置されていた

The sled's runners were frozen tight to the packed-down snow.

そりの滑走部は踏み固められた雪にぴったりと凍りついていた

Men offered two-to-one odds that Buck could not move the sled.

男たちは、バックがそりを動かせなくなる確率は2対1だと主張

A dispute broke out about what "break out" really meant.

「ブレイクアウト」が実際に何を意味するかについて論争が勃発した

O'Brien said Thornton should loosen the sled's frozen base.

オブライエン氏は、ソーントン氏がそりの凍った底を緩めるべきだと述べた

Buck could then "break out" from a solid, motionless start.

すると、バックはしっかりとした静止したスタートから「抜け出す」ことができるのです

Matthewson argued the dog must break the runners free too.

マシューソンさんは、犬もランナーを解放しなければならないと主張した

The men who had heard the bet agreed with Matthewson's view.

その賭けを聞いた男たちはマシューソンの意見に同意した

With that ruling, the odds jumped to three-to-one against Buck.

この判決により、バック氏の不利な状況は3対1に跳ね上がった

No one stepped forward to take the growing three-to-one odds.

3対1の差が拡大する中、誰も前に出ようとしなかった

Not a single man believed Buck could perform the great feat.

バックがその偉業を成し遂げられると信じた者は一人もいなかった

Thornton had been rushed into the bet, heavy with doubts.

ソーントンは強い疑念を抱きながら、賭けに飛び込んだ

Now he looked at the sled and the ten-dog team beside it.

今、彼はそりと、その横の十頭の犬ぞりに目をやった

Seeing the reality of the task made it seem more impossible.

課題の現実を見ると、さらに不可能に思えてきました

Matthewson was full of pride and confidence in that moment.

マシューソンはその瞬間、誇りと自信に満ち溢れていた

"Three to one!" he shouted. "I'll bet another thousand, Thornton!

「三対一だ!」と彼は叫んだ「さらに千ドル賭けてやるよ、ソーントン!」

What do you say?" he added, loud enough for all to hear.

「何と言いますか?」と彼は全員に聞こえるくらい大きな声で付け加えた

Thornton's face showed his doubts, but his spirit had risen.

ソーントンの顔には疑念が浮かんでいたが、彼の精神は高揚していた

That fighting spirit ignored odds and feared nothing at all.

その闘志は逆境をものともせず、何も恐れなかった

He called Hans and Pete to bring all their cash to the table.
彼はハンスとピートに現金を全部テーブルに持ってくるように呼びかけた

They had little left—only two hundred dollars combined.
彼らに残ったのはわずか 200 ドルだけだった

This small sum was their total fortune during hard times.
このわずかな金額が、苦難の時代における彼らの全財産だった

Still, they laid all of the fortune down against Matthewson's bet.
それでも、彼らはマシューソンの賭けに全財産を賭けた

The ten-dog team was unhitched and moved away from the sled.
10頭の犬ぞりは繋ぎが解かれ、そりから離れ去った

Buck was placed in the reins, wearing his familiar harness.
バックはいつもの馬具を着けて手綱を握った

He had caught the energy of the crowd and felt the tension.
彼は群衆のエネルギーを感知し、緊張を感じ取った

Somehow, he knew he had to do something for John Thornton.
どういうわけか、彼はジョン・ソーントンのために何かをしなくてはならないことを知っていました

People murmured with admiration at the dog's proud figure.
人々は犬の誇らしげな姿に感嘆の声をあげた

He was lean and strong, without a single extra ounce of flesh.
彼は痩せていて強健で、余分な肉はひとつもなかった

His full weight of hundred fifty pounds was all power and endurance.
彼の総重量150ポンドはすべて力と持久力でした

Buck's coat gleamed like silk, thick with health and strength.
バックの毛皮は健康と強さで厚く、絹のように輝いていた

The fur along his neck and shoulders seemed to lift and bristle.

首や肩の毛が浮き上がって逆立っているように見えた

His mane moved slightly, each hair alive with his great energy.

彼のたてがみはわずかに動いていて、毛の一本一本が彼の大きなエネルギーで生き生きとしていた

His broad chest and strong legs matched his heavy, tough frame.

彼の広い胸と強い脚は、彼の重くて頑丈な体格によく似合っていた

Muscles rippled under his coat, tight and firm as bound iron.

彼のコートの下で筋肉が波打っており、鉄のように引き締まっていた

Men touched him and swore he was built like a steel machine.

男たちは彼に触れて、彼が鋼鉄の機械のような体格だと断言した

The odds dropped slightly to two to one against the great dog.

偉大な犬に対するオッズはわずかに2対1に下がりました

A man from the Skookum Benches pushed forward, stuttering.

スクーカムベンチの男がどもりながら前に進み出た

"Good, sir! I offer eight hundred for him—before the test, sir!"

「結構です！テスト前なので800ドル差し上げます！」

"Eight hundred, as he stands right now!" the man insisted.

「今の体重だと800キロだ！」男は主張した

Thornton stepped forward, smiled, and shook his head calmly.

ソーントンは前に進み出て微笑み、静かに首を振った

Matthewson quickly stepped in with a warning voice and frown.

マシューソンはすぐに介入し、警告の声を上げて眉をひそめた

"You must step away from him," he said. "Give him space."

「彼から離れなさい」と彼は言った「彼にスペースを与えなさい」

The crowd grew silent; only gamblers still offered two to one.

群衆は静まり返り、ギャンブラーだけがまだ2対1で賭けを申し出ていた

Everyone admired Buck's build, but the load looked too great.

誰もがバックの体格を賞賛したが、荷物が大きすぎるように見えた

Twenty sacks of flour—each fifty pounds in weight—seemed far too much.

小麦粉20袋（各50ポンドの重さ）は多すぎるように思えました

No one was willing to open their pouch and risk their money.

誰もポーチを開けてお金を危険にさらそうとはしませんでした

Thornton knelt beside Buck and took his head in both hands.

ソーントンはバックの横にひざまずき、両手で彼の頭を包んだ

He pressed his cheek against Buck's and spoke into his ear.

彼はバックの頬に自分の頬を押し当てて、耳元で話しかけた

There was no playful shaking or whispered loving insults now.

今では、ふざけて体を揺らしたり、愛を込めてささやき合ったりすることはない

He only murmured softly, "As much as you love me, Buck."

彼はただ小さく呟いた「君が僕を愛しているのと同じくらい、バック」

Buck let out a quiet whine, his eagerness barely restrained.

バックは静かに鳴き声をあげたが、熱意をかろうじて抑えていた

The onlookers watched with curiosity as tension filled the air.

緊張感が漂う中、傍観者たちは好奇心を持って見守った

The moment felt almost unreal, like something beyond reason.

その瞬間は、まるで理屈を超えた何かのようで、ほとんど非現実的に感じられました

When Thornton stood, Buck gently took his hand in his jaws.

ソートンが立ち上がると、バックはそっと彼の手を口の中に入れた

He pressed down with his teeth, then let go slowly and gently.

彼は歯で押さえ、それからゆっくりと優しく離した

It was a silent answer of love, not spoken, but understood.

それは言葉で表現されたものではなく、理解された愛の静かな答えでした

Thornton stepped well back from the dog and gave the signal.

ソートンは犬から十分離れて合図を出した

"Now, Buck," he said, and Buck responded with focused calm.

「さて、バック」と彼は言い、バックは冷静に集中して応えた

Buck tightened the traces, then loosened them by a few inches.

バックは、レールを締め、それから数インチ緩めました

This was the method he had learned; his way to break the sled.

これは彼が学んだ方法であり、そりを壊す彼のやり方だった

"Gee!" Thornton shouted, his voice sharp in the heavy silence.

「おいおい！」ソーントンは重苦しい沈黙の中で鋭い声で叫んだ

Buck turned to the right and lunged with all of his weight.
バックは右に向きを変え、全身全霊で突進した

The slack vanished, and Buck's full mass hit the tight traces.
たるみは消え、バックの全質量がタイトなトレースにぶつかりました

The sled trembled, and the runners made a crisp crackling sound.
そりは震え、ランナーはパリパリという音を立てた

"Haw!" Thornton commanded, shifting Buck's direction again.
「ホー！」ソーントンは再びバックの方向を変えながら命令した

Buck repeated the move, this time pulling sharply to the left.
バックは同じ動きを繰り返し、今度は鋭く左に引いた

The sled cracked louder, the runners snapping and shifting.
そりの音がさらに大きくなり、ランナーがパチンと音を立ててずれた

The heavy load slid slightly sideways across the frozen snow.
重い荷物は凍った雪の上をわずかに横に滑りました

The sled had broken free from the grip of the icy trail!
そりは凍った道のグリップから抜け出しました！

Men held their breath, unaware they were not even breathing.
男たちは息を止めていたが、自分たちが呼吸をしていないことにも気づいていなかった

"Now, PULL!" Thornton cried out across the frozen silence.
「さあ、引け！」凍りついた沈黙の中でソーントンは叫んだ

Thornton's command rang out sharp, like the crack of a whip.
ソーントンの命令は鞭の音のように鋭く響き渡った

Buck hurled himself forward with a fierce and jarring lunge.
バックは激しく、衝撃を与える突進で前方に突進した

His whole frame tensed and bunched for the massive strain.
彼の全身は大きな負担で緊張し、縮こまってしまった

Muscles rippled under his fur like serpents coming alive.
毛皮の下で筋肉が波打っており、蛇が生き返ったようだった

His great chest was low, head stretched forward toward the sled.
彼の大きな胸は低く垂れ下がり、頭はそりに向かって前方に伸びていた

His paws moved like lightning, claws slicing the frozen ground.
彼の足は稲妻のように動き、爪が凍った地面を切り裂いた

Grooves were cut deep as he fought for every inch of traction.
彼が少しでもトラクションを得ようと奮闘するにつれ、溝は深く刻まれていった

The sled rocked, trembled, and began a slow, uneasy motion.
そりは揺れ、震え、ゆっくりと不安定な動きを始めた

One foot slipped, and a man in the crowd groaned aloud.
片足が滑って、群衆の中の男が大きな声でうめき声をあげた

Then the sled lunged forward in a jerking, rough movement.
するとそりはガクガクと激しく動きながら前方に突進した

It didn't stop again—half an inch...an inch...two inches more.
それはまた止まらなかった半インチ、1インチ、さらに2インチ

The jerks became smaller as the sled began to gather speed.
そりがスピードを上げ始めると、揺れは小さくなっていった

Soon Buck was pulling with smooth, even, rolling power.
すぐにバックはスムーズで均一な回転力で牽引するようになりました

Men gasped and finally remembered to breathe again.

男たちは息を呑み、ようやく再び呼吸することを思い出した

They had not noticed their breath had stopped in awe.
彼らは畏怖の念で息が止まっていたことに気づいていなかった

Thornton ran behind, calling out short, cheerful commands.
ソーントンは短く明るい命令を叫びながら後ろを走った

Ahead was a stack of firewood that marked the distance.
前方には距離を示す薪の山がありました

As Buck neared the pile, the cheering grew louder and louder.
バックが山に近づくにつれて、歓声はますます大きくなった

The cheering swelled into a roar as Buck passed the end point.
バックがゴール地点を通過すると、歓声は大音響にまで高まった

Men jumped and shouted, even Matthewson broke into a grin.
男たちは飛び上がって叫び、マシューソン氏さえも笑顔を見せた

Hats flew into the air, mittens were tossed without thought or aim.
帽子は空に舞い、手袋は考えも目的もなく投げられた

Men grabbed each other and shook hands without knowing who.
男たちは、誰とも知らずに、互いに掴み合って握手をした

The whole crowd buzzed in wild, joyful celebration.
群衆全体が熱狂的な喜びの祝賀でざわめいた

Thornton dropped to his knees beside Buck with trembling hands.
ソーントンは震える手でバックの横にひざまずいた

He pressed his head to Buck's and shook him gently back and forth.

彼はバックの頭に自分の頭を押し当てて、優しく前後に揺さぶった

Those who approached heard him curse the dog with quiet love.

近づいた人々は、彼が静かに愛情を込めて犬を呪うのを聞いた

He swore at Buck for a long time—softly, warmly, with emotion.

彼はバックに向かって長い間、優しく、熱く、感情を込めて罵り続けた

"Good, sir! Good, sir!" cried the Skookum Bench king in a rush.

「よかったです！よかったです！」スクーカムベンチの王は慌てて叫んだ

"I'll give you a thousand—no, twelve hundred—for that dog, sir!"

「その犬に1000ドル、いえ、1200ドルお支払いします！」

Thornton rose slowly to his feet, his eyes shining with emotion.

ソーントンは感情に輝いた目でゆっくりと立ち上がった

Tears streamed openly down his cheeks without any shame.

彼の頬には恥ずかしげもなく涙が流れ落ちた

"Sir," he said to the Skookum Bench king, steady and firm

「閣下」彼はスクーカムベンチキングに、落ち着いて毅然と言った

"No, sir. You can go to hell, sir. That's my final answer."

「いいえ地獄に落ちてくださいこれが私の最終的な答えです」

Buck grabbed Thornton's hand gently in his strong jaws.

バックは力強い顎でソーントンの手を優しく掴んだ

Thornton shook him playfully, their bond deep as ever.

ソーントンは彼をふざけて揺さぶったが、二人の絆は相変わらず深かった

The crowd, moved by the moment, stepped back in silence.

群衆はその瞬間に感動し、静かに後ずさりした

From then on, none dared interrupt such sacred affection.
それ以来、誰もそのような神聖な愛情を邪魔しようとは
しなかった

The Sound of the Call
呼び声の音

Buck had earned sixteen hundred dollars in five minutes.
バックは5分間で1600ドルを稼いだ
The money let John Thornton pay off some of his debts.
そのお金でジョン・ソーントンは借金の一部を返済する
ことができた
With the rest of the money he headed East with his partners.
残りのお金を持って、彼は仲間とともに東へ向かった
They sought a fabled lost mine, as old as the country itself.
彼らは、国自体と同じくらい古い、伝説の失われた鉱山
を探していました
Many men had looked for the mine, but few had ever found
it.
多くの人が鉱山を探したが、発見できた人はほとんどい
なかった
More than a few men had vanished during the dangerous
quest.
危険な探索中に行方不明になった男も少なくなかった
This lost mine was wrapped in both mystery and old
tragedy.
この失われた鉱山は謎と昔の悲劇に包まれていました
No one knew who the first man to find the mine had been.
鉱山を最初に発見した人が誰であったかは誰も知らなか
った
The oldest stories don't mention anyone by name.

最も古い物語には誰の名前も出てきません

There had always been an ancient ramshackle cabin there.

そこには古くて荒れ果てた小屋がずっとあった

Dying men had sworn there was a mine next to that old cabin.

死にゆく男たちは、その古い小屋の隣に地雷があると断言した

They proved their stories with gold like none found elsewhere.

彼らは、他では見つからないような金で自分たちの話を証明した

No living soul had ever looted the treasure from that place.

これまで、その場所から宝物を略奪した者は誰もいなかった

The dead were dead, and dead men tell no tales.

死者は死んだそして死者は何も語らない

So Thornton and his friends headed into the East.

そこでソーントンとその友人たちは東へ向かった

Pete and Hans joined, bringing Buck and six strong dogs.

ピートとハンスもバックと6匹の強い犬を連れて参加しました

They set off down an unknown trail where others had failed.

彼らは、他の人々が失敗した未知の道を歩み始めた

They sledded seventy miles up the frozen Yukon River.

彼らは凍ったユーコン川を70マイルそりで遡った

They turned left and followed the trail into the Stewart.

彼らは左に曲がり、道を辿ってスチュワートへと入った

They passed the Mayo and McQuestion, pressing farther on.

彼らはメイヨーとマククエスチョンを通過し、さらに前進した

The Stewart shrank into a stream, threading jagged peaks.

スチュワート川は、ギザギザの峰々を縫うように流れながら、縮小していった

These sharp peaks marked the very spine of the continent.

これらの鋭い峰々はまさに大陸の背骨を形作っています

John Thornton demanded little from men or the wild land.
ジョン・ソーントンは人間や荒野にほとんど何も要求しなかった

He feared nothing in nature and faced the wild with ease.
彼は自然の中で何も恐れることなく、野生に気楽に立ち向かった

With only salt and a rifle, he could travel where he wished.
塩とライフル銃だけを持って、彼は望むところへ旅することができた

Like the natives, he hunted food while he journeyed along.
原住民たちと同じように、彼は旅をしながら食べ物を狩りました

If he caught nothing, he kept going, trusting luck ahead.
何も釣れなかったら、彼は幸運を祈って進み続けた

On this long journey, meat was the main thing they ate.
この長い旅の間、彼らが主に食べたのは肉でした

The sled held tools and ammo, but no strict timetable.
そりには道具や弾薬が積まれていたが、厳密なスケジュールはなかった

Buck loved this wandering; the endless hunt and fishing.
バックはこの放浪、終わりのない狩りと釣りを愛していた

For weeks they were traveling day after steady day.
彼らは何週間も毎日休みなく旅を続けた

Other times they made camps and stayed still for weeks.
時にはキャンプを張って何週間もじっと留まることもあった

The dogs rested while the men dug through frozen dirt.
男たちが凍った土を掘っている間、犬たちは休んでいた

They warmed pans over fires and searched for hidden gold.
彼らは火で鍋を温め、隠された金を探しました

Some days they starved, and some days they had feasts.
ある日彼らは飢え、ある日はごちそうを食べました

Their meals depended on the game and the luck of the hunt.
彼らの食事は獲物と狩りの運次第だった

When summer came, men and dogs packed loads on their backs.
夏になると、男たちと犬たちは背中に荷物を詰め込んだ

They rafted across blue lakes hidden in mountain forests.
彼らは山の森に隠れた青い湖をラフティングで渡りました

They sailed slim boats on rivers no man had ever mapped.
彼らは、誰も地図に描いたことのない川を細長い船で航海した

Those boats were built from trees they sawed in the wild.
これらのボートは野生で伐採した木から造られました

The months passed, and they twisted through the wild unknown lands.
数ヶ月が過ぎ、彼らは未知の荒野を旅した

There were no men there, yet old traces hinted that men had been.
そこには男はいなかったが、古い痕跡が男がいたことを暗示していた

If the Lost Cabin was real, then others had once come this way.
もし「失われた小屋」が実在するのなら、かつて他の人々もこの道を通ってきたことになる

They crossed high passes in blizzards, even during the summer.
彼らは夏でも吹雪の中、高い峠を越えた

They shivered under the midnight sun on bare mountain slopes.
彼らは裸の山の斜面で真夜中の太陽の下、震えていた

Between the treeline and the snowfields, they climbed slowly.
森林限界と雪原の間を彼らはゆっくりと登っていった

In warm valleys, they swatted at clouds of gnats and flies.
暖かい谷間では、彼らはブヨやハエの大群を叩き落としました

They picked sweet berries near glaciers in full summer bloom.

彼らは真夏に花を咲かせた氷河の近くで甘いベリーを摘みました

The flowers they found were as lovely as those in the Southland.

彼らが見つけた花は、南部の花と同じくらい美しかった

That fall they reached a lonely region filled with silent lakes.

その秋、彼らは静かな湖が広がる寂しい地域に到着した

The land was sad and empty, once alive with birds and beasts.

かつては鳥や獣たちが生きていたこの地は、悲しく空虚な場所でした

Now there was no life, just the wind and ice forming in pools.

今では生命は存在せず、ただ風と水たまりに形成される氷だけが存在していました

Waves lapped against empty shores with a soft, mournful sound.

波は柔らかく悲しげな音を立てながら、誰もいない海岸に打ち寄せた

Another winter came, and they followed faint, old trails again.

再び冬が来て、彼らは再びかすかな古い道をたどりました

These were the trails of men who had searched long before them.

これらは、彼らよりずっと前に捜索していた人々の足跡でした

Once they found a path cut deep into the dark forest.

彼らはかつて暗い森の奥深くに切り込まれた道を見つけました

It was an old trail, and they felt the lost cabin was close.

それは古い道であり、彼らは失われた小屋が近いと感じました

But the trail led nowhere and faded into the thick woods.

しかし、道はどこにも通じず、深い森の中に消えていった

Whoever made the trail, and why they made it, no one knew.

誰がその道を作ったのか、そしてなぜ作ったのかは誰も知らなかった

Later, they found the wreck of a lodge hidden among the trees.

その後、彼らは木々の間に隠れたロッジの残骸を発見した

Rotting blankets lay scattered where someone once had slept.

かつて誰かが寝ていた場所には、腐った毛布が散乱していた

John Thornton found a long-barreled flintlock buried inside.

ジョン・ソーントンは、中に埋められていた長い銃身のフリントロック式銃を発見した

He knew this was a Hudson Bay gun from early trading days.

彼は取引の初期の頃からこれがハドソン湾の銃であることを知っていた

In those days such guns were traded for stacks of beaver skins.

当時、そのような銃は大量のビーバーの皮と交換されていました

That was all—no clue remained of the man who built the lodge.

それがすべてだったロッジを建てた男についての手がかりは何一つ残っていなかった

Spring came again, and they found no sign of the Lost Cabin.

再び春が来たが、彼らは失われた小屋の痕跡を見つけられなかった

Instead they found a broad valley with a shallow stream.
代わりに彼らは浅い小川のある広い谷を見つけました

Gold lay across the pan bottoms like smooth, yellow butter.
金は滑らかな黄色いバターのように鍋の底に広がっていました

They stopped there and searched no farther for the cabin.
彼らはそこで立ち止まり、それ以上小屋を捜すことはしなかった

Each day they worked and found thousands in gold dust.
彼らは毎日働いて何千もの金粉を発見しました

They packed the gold in bags of moose-hide, fifty pounds each.
彼らは金貨をヘラジカの皮の袋にそれぞれ50ポンドずつ詰めた

The bags were stacked like firewood outside their small lodge.
彼らの小さな小屋の外に、袋が薪のように積み上げられていた

They worked like giants, and the days passed like quick dreams.
彼らは巨人のように働き、日々はあっという間に夢のように過ぎていった

They heaped up treasure as the endless days rolled swiftly by.
終わりのない日々があっという間に過ぎていくなか、彼らは宝物を積み上げていった

There was little for the dogs to do except haul meat now and then.
時々肉を運ぶ以外、犬達にやることはほとんどなかった

Thornton hunted and killed the game, and Buck lay by the fire.
ソーントンは獲物を狩って殺し、バックは火のそばに横たわっていた

He spent long hours in silence, lost in thought and memory.

彼は長い時間を沈黙の中で過ごし、考えや記憶に浸って
いた

The image of the hairy man came more often into Buck's
mind.
毛深い男のイメージがバックの心の中に頻繁に浮かんだ

Now that work was scarce, Buck dreamed while blinking at
the fire.
仕事がほとんどなくなったので、バックは火を見つめな
がら夢を見ていた

In those dreams, Buck wandered with the man in another
world.
夢の中で、バックはその男とともに別の世界をさまよっ
ていた

Fear seemed the strongest feeling in that distant world.
その遠い世界では恐怖が最も強い感情であるように思え
た

Buck saw the hairy man sleep with his head bowed low.
バックは毛深い男が頭を低く下げて眠っているのを見た

His hands were clasped, and his sleep was restless and
broken.
彼は両手を握りしめており、眠りは不安定で中断されて
いた

He used to wake with a start and stare fearfully into the
dark.
彼はいつもびっくりして目を覚まし、恐怖に怯えながら
暗闇を見つめていた

Then he'd toss more wood onto the fire to keep the flame
bright.
それから彼は炎を明るく保つためにさらに木を火に投げ
入れました

Sometimes they walked along a beach by a gray, endless sea.
時々彼らは灰色の果てしない海のそばの浜辺を歩いた

The hairy man picked shellfish and ate them as he walked.
毛深い男は歩きながら貝を摘んで食べた

His eyes searched always for hidden dangers in the
shadows.

彼の目は常に影に隠れた危険を探し求めていた

His legs were always ready to sprint at the first sign of threat.

彼の足は、脅威を感じた瞬間にすぐに走れる準備ができていた

They crept through the forest, silent and wary, side by side.

彼らは静かに、用心深く、並んで森の中を進んでいった

Buck followed at his heels, and both of them stayed alert.

バックは彼の後を追ったが、二人とも警戒を怠らなかった

Their ears twitched and moved, their noses sniffed the air.

彼らの耳はぴくぴくと動き、鼻は空気を嗅ぎました

The man could hear and smell the forest as sharply as Buck.

男はバックと同じくらい鋭く森の音を聞き、匂いを嗅ぐことができた

The hairy man swung through the trees with sudden speed.

毛深い男は突然のスピードで木々の間を飛び越えた

He leapt from branch to branch, never missing his grip.

彼はつかんだものを一度も逃さず、枝から枝へと飛び移った

He moved as fast above the ground as he did upon it.

彼は地上で動くのと同じくらい速く地上でも動いた

Buck remembered long nights beneath the trees, keeping watch.

バックは木々の下で監視をしていた長い夜を思い出した

The man slept roosting in the branches, clinging tight.

男はしっかりと枝にしがみついて眠った

This vision of the hairy man was tied closely to the deep call.

この毛深い男の幻影は深い呼び声と密接に結びついていました

The call still sounded through the forest with haunting force.

その呼び声は今も忘れがたい力で森中に響き渡っていた

The call filled Buck with longing and a restless sense of joy.

その電話はバックを憧れと落ち着かない喜びで満たした

He felt strange urges and stirrings that he could not name.
彼は、名前のつけられない奇妙な衝動と興奮を感じた

Sometimes he followed the call deep into the quiet woods.
時々彼はその呼び声に従って静かな森の奥深くまで行った

He searched for the calling, barking softly or sharply as he went.
彼は呼び声を探しながら、歩きながら小さく、あるいは鋭く吠えた

He sniffed the moss and black soil where the grasses grew.
彼は草が生えている苔や黒い土を嗅ぎました

He snorted with delight at the rich smells of the deep earth.
彼は深い土の豊かな香りに大喜びで鼻を鳴らした

He crouched for hours behind trunks covered in fungus.
彼は菌類に覆われた幹の後ろに何時間もしゃがんでいた

He stayed still, listening wide-eyed to every tiny sound.
彼はじっとしたまま、目を大きく開いてあらゆる小さな音に耳を傾けていた

He may have hoped to surprise the thing that gave the call.
彼は電話をかけてきたものを驚かせたいと思ったのかもしれない

He did not know why he acted this way—he simply did.
彼はなぜこのような行動をとったのか知らなかったが、ただそうしただけだった

The urges came from deep within, beyond thought or reason.
その衝動は思考や理性を超えて、心の奥底から湧き上がってきたのです

Irresistible urges took hold of Buck without warning or reason.
警告も理由もなく、抑えられない衝動がバックを襲った

At times he was dozing lazily in camp under the midday heat.
彼は時々、真昼の暑さの中、キャンプで怠惰にうとうとしていた

Suddenly, his head lifted and his ears shoot up alert.

突然、彼は頭を上げ、耳を警戒した

Then he sprang up and dash into the wild without pause.
それから彼は跳び上がり、立ち止まることなく荒野へと
駆け出した

He ran for hours through forest paths and open spaces.
彼は森の小道や広場を何時間も走り続けた

He loved to follow dry creek beds and spy on birds in the trees.
彼は乾いた小川の川床を歩き回ったり、木々にとまる鳥
を観察するのが大好きでした

He could lie hidden all day, watching partridges strut around.
彼は一日中隠れて、ヤマウズラが歩き回るのを眺めてい
た

They drummed and marched, unaware of Buck's still presence.
彼らはバックがまだそこにいることに気づかず、太鼓を
鳴らしながら行進した

But what he loved most was running at twilight in summer.
しかし、彼が最も好きだったのは、夏の夕暮れ時に走る
ことだった

The dim light and sleepy forest sounds filled him with joy.
薄暗い光と眠たげな森の音が彼を喜びで満たした

He read the forest signs as clearly as a man reads a book.
彼は人が本を読むのと同じくらいはっきりと森の標識を
読み取った

And he searched always for the strange thing that called him.
そして彼は、自分を呼ぶ奇妙なものを常に探していた

That calling never stopped—it reached him waking or sleeping.
その呼びかけは決して止むことはなく、目覚めていると
きも眠っているときも彼に届きました

One night, he woke with a start, eyes sharp and ears high.

ある夜、彼はハッと目を覚まし、目を鋭くし、耳を高く上げました

His nostrils twitched as his mane stood bristling in waves.
たてがみが波打つように逆立ち、鼻孔がぴくぴく動いた

From deep in the forest came the sound again, the old call.
森の奥深くから、また古い呼び声が聞こえてきた

This time the sound rang clearly, a long, haunting, familiar howl.
今度はその音がはっきりと響いた長く、忘れられない、聞き慣れた遠吠えだった

It was like a husky's cry, but strange and wild in tone.
それはハスキーの鳴き声のようでしたが、奇妙で野性的な音色でした

Buck knew the sound at once—he had heard the exact sound long ago.
バックはその音をすぐに理解したずっと前にまったく同じ音を聞いたことがあるのだ

He leapt through camp and vanished swiftly into the woods.
彼はキャンプを飛び越えて森の中へ素早く姿を消した

As he neared the sound, he slowed and moved with care.
音が聞こえる方向に近づくと、彼は速度を落とし、慎重に動いた

Soon he reached a clearing between thick pine trees.
やがて彼は松の木々が生い茂る空き地に到着した

There, upright on its haunches, sat a tall, lean timber wolf.
そこには、背が高くて痩せたタイリクオオカミが、お尻を上げて座っていました

The wolf's nose pointed skyward, still echoing the call.
狼の鼻は空を向いて、まだ呼び声を反響させていた

Buck had made no sound, yet the wolf stopped and listened.
雄鹿は音を立てなかったが、オオカミは立ち止まって耳を澄ませた

Sensing something, the wolf tensed, searching the darkness.
何かを感じて、狼は緊張し、暗闇の中を探し始めた

Buck crept into view, body low, feet quiet on the ground.

雄鹿は体を低くし、足を地面に静かにつけたまま、こっそりと視界に入ってきた

His tail was straight, his body coiled tight with tension.
彼の尻尾はまっすぐで、体は緊張で固く縮こまっていた

He showed both threat and a kind of rough friendship.
彼は脅迫と一種の荒っぽい友情の両方を示した

It was the wary greeting shared by beasts of the wild.
それは野生の獣たちが交わす警戒心の強い挨拶だった

But the wolf turned and fled as soon as it saw Buck.
しかし、オオカミはバックを見るとすぐに向きを変えて逃げてしまいました

Buck gave chase, leaping wildly, eager to overtake it.
雄鹿は追いかけ、激しく跳躍し、追いかけようとした

He followed the wolf into a dry creek blocked by a timber jam.
彼はオオカミを追って、木材の詰まりで塞がれた乾いた小川へと入った

Cornered, the wolf spun around and stood its ground.
追い詰められた狼はくるりと向きを変え、その場に立ち尽くした

The wolf snarled and snapped like a trapped husky dog in a fight.
狼は、戦いで捕らえられたハスキー犬のように唸り声をあげ、噛みついた

The wolf's teeth clicked fast, its body bristling with wild fury.
狼の歯がカチカチと音を立て、その体は激しい怒りで逆立った

Buck did not attack but circled the wolf with careful friendliness.
雄鹿は攻撃はせず、慎重に友好的にオオカミの周りを回った

He tried to block his escape by slow, harmless movements.
彼はゆっくりとした無害な動きで逃走を阻止しようとした

The wolf was wary and scared—Buck outweighed him three times.

オオカミは警戒して怖がっていましたバックの体重はオオカミの3倍もあったからです

The wolf's head barely reached up to Buck's massive shoulder.

狼の頭はかろうじてバックの大きな肩に届いた

Watching for a gap, the wolf bolted and the chase began again.

隙を狙ってオオカミは逃げ出し、追跡が再び始まった

Several times Buck cornered him, and the dance repeated.

バックは何度か彼を追い詰め、ダンスを繰り返した

The wolf was thin and weak, or Buck could not have caught him.

オオカミは痩せて弱かったので、バックが捕まえることはできなかったでしょう

Each time Buck drew near, the wolf spun and faced him in fear.

バックが近づくたびに、オオカミは回転して恐怖に怯えながら彼の方を向いた

Then at the first chance, he dashed off into the woods once more.

そして、最初のチャンスを逃さず、彼は再び森の中へ駆け出した

But Buck did not give up, and finally the wolf came to trust him.

しかしバックは諦めず、ついにオオカミは彼を信頼するようになりました

He sniffed Buck's nose, and the two grew playful and alert.

彼はバックの鼻を嗅ぎ、二人は遊び心と警戒心を持つようになった

They played like wild animals, fierce yet shy in their joy.

彼らは喜びの中にも勇ましさ、恥ずかしさを感じながら、野生動物のように遊んでいました

After a while, the wolf trotted off with calm purpose.

しばらくして、オオカミは落ち着いた様子で小走りに去っていきました

He clearly showed Buck that he meant to be followed.
彼は明らかにバックに、尾行されるつもりである事を示した

They ran side by side through the twilight gloom.
彼らは夕暮れの薄暗い中を並んで走った

They followed the creek bed up into the rocky gorge.
彼らは小川の流れに沿って岩だらけの峡谷まで登っていった

They crossed a cold divide where the stream had begun.
彼らは川が流れ始めた冷たい分水嶺を越えた

On the far slope they found wide forest and many streams.
向こうの斜面には広い森とたくさんの小川がありました

Through this vast land, they ran for hours without stopping.
彼らはこの広大な土地を何時間も止まることなく走り続けた

The sun rose higher, the air grew warm, but they ran on.
太陽は高く昇り、空気は暖かくなったが、彼らは走り続けた

Buck was filled with joy—he knew he was answering his calling.
バックは喜びに満たされた彼は自分の使命に応えているのだと悟ったのだ

He ran beside his forest brother, closer to the call's source.
彼は森の兄弟の横を走り、その声の源に近づいた

Old feelings returned, powerful and hard to ignore.
昔の感情が戻ってきましたそれは強力で無視できないものでした

These were the truths behind the memories from his dreams.
これらは彼の夢の記憶の背後にある真実だった

He had done all this before in a distant and shadowy world.
彼はこれまでにも、遠く離れた暗い世界でこのすべてをやってきた

Now he did this again, running wild with the open sky above.

今、彼は再びこれを実行し、頭上の広い空に向かって暴れ回った

They stopped at a stream to drink from the cold flowing water.
彼らは小川のそばに立ち止まり、冷たい流れ水を飲みました

As he drank, Buck suddenly remembered John Thornton.
酒を飲みながら、バックは突然ジョン・ソーントンのことを思い出した

He sat down in silence, torn by the pull of loyalty and the calling.
彼は忠誠心と使命感に引き裂かれながら、黙って座っていた

The wolf trotted on, but came back to urge Buck forward.
オオカミは小走りで進みましたが、戻ってきてバックを促しました

He sniffed his nose and tried to coax him with soft gestures.
彼は鼻をすすりながら、優しい仕草で彼をなだめようとした

But Buck turned around and started back the way he came.
しかしバックは向きを変えて来た道を戻り始めた

The wolf ran beside him for a long time, whining quietly.
狼は静かに鳴きながら、長い間彼のそばを走り続けました

Then he sat down, raised his nose, and let out a long howl.
それから彼は座り、鼻を上げて、長い遠吠えをしました

It was a mournful cry, softening as Buck walked away.
それは悲しげな叫びだったが、バックが立ち去ると声は小さくなっていった

Buck listened as the sound of the cry faded slowly into the forest silence.
バックは、叫び声が森の静寂の中にゆっくりと消えていくのを聞いていた

John Thornton was eating dinner when Buck burst into the camp.

ジョン・ソーントンが夕食を食べていると、バックがキャンプに飛び込んできた

Buck leapt upon him wildly, licking, biting, and tumbling him.

バックは激しく彼に飛びかかり、舐めたり、噛んだり、転がしたりした

He knocked him over, scrambled on top, and kissed his face.

彼は彼を倒し、上に登り、彼の顔にキスをした

Thornton called this "playing the general tom-fool" with affection.

ソーントンはこれを愛情を込めて「大将の愚か者を演じる」と呼んだ

All the while, he cursed Buck gently and shook him back and forth.

その間ずっと、彼はバックを優しく罵りながら、彼を前後に揺さぶり続けた

For two whole days and nights, Buck never left the camp once.

丸二日二晩、バックは一度もキャンプを離れなかった

He kept close to Thornton and never let him out of his sight.

彼はソーントンのすぐそばにいて、決して彼から目を離さなかった

He followed him as he worked and watched him while he ate.

彼は彼が仕事をしている間、後をついて歩き、彼が食事をしている間、見守っていた

He saw Thornton into his blankets at night and out each morning.

彼はソーントンが夜になると毛布にくるまり、毎朝毛布から出てくるのを見ていた

But soon the forest call returned, louder than ever before.

しかし、すぐに森の呼び声が、以前よりも大きな声で戻ってきました

Buck grew restless again, stirred by thoughts of the wild wolf.

バックは野生の狼のことを考えて再び落ち着かなくなった

He remembered the open land and running side by side.
彼は広い土地と並んで走っていたことを思い出した

He began wandering into the forest once more, alone and alert.
彼は再び、一人で用心深く森の中を歩き始めた

But the wild brother did not return, and the howl was not heard.
しかし、野生の兄弟は戻ってこなかったし、遠吠えも聞こえなかった

Buck started sleeping outside, staying away for days at a time.
バックは一度に何日も離れて外で寝るようになりました

Once he crossed the high divide where the creek had begun.
かつて彼は小川が始まる高い分水嶺を越えた

He entered the land of dark timber and wide flowing streams.
彼は暗い森と広く流れる小川の土地に入った

For a week he roamed, searching for signs of the wild brother.
彼は一週間、野生の兄弟の痕跡を探して歩き回った

He killed his own meat and travelled with long, tireless strides.
彼は自分で肉を殺し、疲れることなく長い歩幅で旅を続けた

He fished for salmon in a wide river that reached the sea.
彼は海に通じる広い川で鮭を釣った

There, he fought and killed a black bear maddened by bugs.
そこで彼は虫に狂ったアメリカグマと闘って殺した

The bear had been fishing and ran blindly through the trees.
クマは魚釣りをしていて、木々の間を盲目的に走り回っていました

The battle was a fierce one, waking Buck's deep fighting spirit up.

戦いは激しいものとなり、バックの根深い闘志が目覚めた

Two days later, Buck returned to find wolverines at his kill.
2日後、バックは獲物を捕らえて戻ってきたが、そこにはクズリがいた

A dozen of them quarreled over the meat in noisy fury.
彼らのうちの12人が、肉をめぐって騒々しく口論した

Buck charged and scattered them like leaves in the wind.
バックは突撃し、彼らを風に舞う木の葉のように散らばらせた

Two wolves remained behind—silent, lifeless, and unmoving forever.
2匹のオオカミが後ろに残りました沈黙し、生気もなく、永遠に動かずにいました

The thirst for blood grew stronger than ever.
血への渇望はこれまで以上に強くなった

Buck was a hunter, a killer, feeding off living creatures.
バックはハンターであり、殺人者であり、生き物を食べて生きていました

He survived alone, relying on his strength and sharp senses.
彼は自分の力と鋭い感覚を頼りに、一人で生き延びた

He thrived in the wild, where only the toughest could live.
彼は、最もタフな者だけが生きられる野生の中で繁栄した

From this, a great pride rose up and filled Buck's whole being.
このことから、大きな誇りが湧き上がり、バックの全身を満たした

His pride showed in his every step, in the ripple of every muscle.
彼の誇りは、一歩一歩、筋肉の動き一つ一つに表れていた

His pride was as clear as speech, seen in how he carried himself.
彼の態度を見れば、彼の誇りが言葉ではっきりと伝わってきた

Even his thick coat looked more majestic and gleamed brighter.

彼の厚い毛皮もより威厳を増し、より明るく輝いて見えました

Buck could have been mistaken for a giant timber wolf.

バックは巨大なタイリクオオカミと間違われる可能性もあった

Except for brown on his muzzle and spots above his eyes.

鼻先の茶色と目の上の斑点を除いて

And the white streak of fur that ran down the middle of his chest.

そして、胸の真ん中に走る白い毛の筋

He was even larger than the biggest wolf of that fierce breed.

彼は、その獰猛な種族の最大のオオカミよりもさらに大きかった

His father, a St. Bernard, gave him size and heavy frame.

彼の父親はセント・バーナード犬で、彼は体格が大きく、がっしりとした体格でした

His mother, a shepherd, shaped that bulk into wolf-like form.

羊飼いであった彼の母親は、その巨体を狼のような形に整えました

He had the long muzzle of a wolf, though heavier and broader.

彼はオオカミのような長い鼻先を持っていたが、オオカミよりも重く、幅広だった

His head was a wolf's, but built on a massive, majestic scale.

彼の頭は狼の頭だったが、巨大で荘厳なスケールの上に造られていた

Buck's cunning was the cunning of the wolf and of the wild.

バックの狡猾さはオオカミと野生の狡猾さと同じだった

His intelligence came from both the German Shepherd and St. Bernard.

彼の知性はジャーマン・シェパードとセント・バーナードの両方から受け継がれました

All this, plus harsh experience, made him a fearsome creature.

これらすべてと厳しい経験が彼を恐ろしい生き物にしたのです

He was as formidable as any beast that roamed the northern wild.

彼は北の荒野をさまようどんな獣にも劣らず恐ろしい存在だった

Living only on meat, Buck reached the full peak of his strength.

肉だけを食べて生きたバックは、その強さの頂点に達した

He overflowed with power and male force in every fiber of him.

彼は全身から力と男性的な力があふれていた

When Thornton stroked his back, the hairs sparked with energy.

ソーントンが背中を撫でると、毛がエネルギーに満ちて火花を散らした

Each hair crackled, charged with the touch of living magnetism.

髪の毛の一本一本が、生きた磁力の感触を帯びてパチパチと音を立てた

His body and brain were tuned to the finest possible pitch.

彼の体と脳は可能な限り最高の調子に調整されていました

Every nerve, fiber, and muscle worked in perfect harmony.

すべての神経、繊維、筋肉が完璧な調和で機能しました

To any sound or sight needing action, he responded instantly.

行動を必要とするあらゆる音や光景に対して、彼は即座に反応しました

If a husky leaped to attack, Buck could leap twice as fast.

ハスキー犬が攻撃するために飛びかかると、バックは2倍の速さで飛びかかることができます

He reacted quicker than others could even see or hear.

彼は他の人が見たり聞いたりするよりも早く反応した

Perception, decision, and action all came in one fluid moment.

認識、決断、行動のすべてが流れるような瞬間に起こりました

In truth, these acts were separate, but too fast to notice.

実際には、これらの行為は別々でしたが、あまりにも速すぎて気づかなかったのです

So brief were the gaps between these acts, they seemed as one.

これらの行為の間の間隔は非常に短かったので、それらは一つの行為のように見えました

His muscles and being was like tightly coiled springs.

彼の筋肉と体格は、きつく巻かれたバネのようでした

His body surged with life, wild and joyful in its power.

彼の体は生命力に満ち溢れ、その力は野性的で喜びに満ちていた

At times he felt like the force was going to burst out of him entirely.

時々、彼はその力が完全に自分から噴き出してしまうように感じた

"Never was there such a dog," Thornton said one quiet day.

「こんな犬は今までいなかったよ」とソーントンは静かなある日に言った

The partners watched Buck striding proudly from the camp.

パートナーたちはバックがキャンプから誇らしげに歩いてくるのを見守った

"When he was made, he changed what a dog can be," said Pete.

「彼が生まれたとき、犬の可能性は大きく変わりました」とピートさんは語った

"By Jesus! I think so myself," Hans quickly agreed.

「イエスに誓って！私もそう思います」ハンスはすぐに同意しました

They saw him march off, but not the change that came after.

彼らは彼が行進するのを見たが、その後に起こる変化は見なかった

As soon as he entered the woods, Buck transformed completely.

森に入るとすぐに、バックは完全に変身しました

He no longer marched, but moved like a wild ghost among trees.

彼はもう行進せず、木々の間を野生の幽霊のように動いた

He became silent, cat-footed, a flicker passing through shadows.

彼は黙り、猫足になり、影の中をちらちらと通り過ぎるようになった

He used cover with skill, crawling on his belly like a snake.

彼は蛇のように腹ばいで這い、巧みに身を隠した

And like a snake, he could leap forward and strike in silence.

そして蛇のように、静かに前に飛び出し攻撃することができた

He could steal a ptarmigan straight from its hidden nest.

彼はライチョウを隠れた巣から直接盗むこともできる

He killed sleeping rabbits without a single sound.

彼は音も立てずに眠っているウサギを殺した

He could catch chipmunks midair as they fled too slowly.

彼は、逃げるのが遅すぎるシマリスを空中で捕まえることができました

Even fish in pools could not escape his sudden strikes.

池の中の魚さえも彼の突然の攻撃から逃れることはできなかった

Not even clever beavers fixing dams were safe from him.

ダムを建設する賢いビーバーでさえ彼から逃れることはできませんでした

He killed for food, not for fun—but liked his own kills best.

彼は楽しみのためではなく、食べるために殺したが、自分が殺すのが一番好きだった

Still, a sly humor ran through some of his silent hunts.

それでも、彼の静かな狩りの中には、狡猾なユーモアが流れていた

He crept up close to squirrels, only to let them escape.
彼はリスに忍び寄ったが、結局逃げられてしまった

They were going to flee to the trees, chattering in fearful outrage.
彼らは、恐怖と怒りに震えながら、木々に向かって逃げようとしていました

As fall came, moose began to appear in greater numbers.
秋になると、ヘラジカの出現数が増え始めました

They moved slowly into the low valleys to meet the winter.
彼らは冬を迎えるためにゆっくりと低い谷間へと移動した

Buck had already brought down one young, stray calf.
バックはすでに、迷い子牛を一頭仕留めていた

But he longed to face larger, more dangerous prey.
しかし彼は、もっと大きくて危険な獲物に立ち向かうことを切望していた

One day on the divide, at the creek's head, he found his chance.
ある日、分水嶺の小川の源流で、彼はチャンスを見つけた

A herd of twenty moose had crossed from forested lands.
20頭のヘラジカの群れが森林地帯から渡ってきた

Among them was a mighty bull; the leader of the group.
彼らの中には、群れのリーダーである力強い雄牛がいました

The bull stood over six feet tall and looked fierce and wild.
その雄牛は身長が6フィート以上あり、獰猛で野性的に見える

He tossed his wide antlers, fourteen points branching outward.
彼は14本の先端が外側に枝分かれした幅広い角を投げた

The tips of those antlers stretched seven feet across.
その角の先端は幅7フィートに伸びていました

His small eyes burned with rage as he spotted Buck nearby.

近くにバックがいるのを見つけると、彼の小さな目は怒りで燃え上がった
He let out a furious roar, trembling with fury and pain.
彼は怒りと苦痛に震えながら、激しい叫び声を上げた
An arrow-end stuck out near his flank, feathered and sharp.
彼の脇腹近くには、羽根の生えた鋭い矢尻が突き出ていた
This wound helped explain his savage, bitter mood.
この傷は彼の残忍で苦々しい気分を説明するのに役立った
Buck, guided by ancient hunting instinct, made his move.
バックは、古代の狩猟本能に導かれて行動を起こした
He aimed to separate the bull from the rest of the herd.
彼は雄牛を群れの残りから分離することを目指した
This was no easy task—it took speed and fierce cunning.
これは決して簡単な仕事ではありませんでしたスピードと鋭い狡猾さが必要でした
He barked and danced near the bull, just out of range.
彼は雄牛の射程範囲外で、雄牛の近くで吠えて踊りました
The moose lunged with huge hooves and deadly antlers.
ヘラジカは巨大なひずめと致命的な角で突進してきました
One blow could have ended Buck's life in a heartbeat.
一撃でバックの命は一瞬で終わっていたかもしれない
Unable to leave the threat behind, the bull grew mad.
脅威から逃れられず、雄牛は激怒した
He charged in fury, but Buck always slipped away.
彼は激怒して突進したが、バックはいつも逃げ去った
Buck faked weakness, luring him farther from the herd.
バックは弱さを装い、彼を群れから遠ざけようと誘い出しました
But young bulls were going to charge back to protect the leader.
しかし若い雄牛たちはリーダーを守るために突撃しようとしていた

They forced Buck to retreat and the bull to rejoin the group.
彼らはバックを退却させ、雄牛を群れに復帰させた

There is a patience in the wild, deep and unstoppable.
野生には、深くて止めることのできない忍耐力がある

A spider waits motionless in its web for countless hours.
蜘蛛は巣の中で何時間も動かずに待ちます

A snake coils without twitching, and waits till it is time.
蛇はぴくぴくせずにとぐろを巻いて、時が来るまで待ちます

A panther lies in ambush, until the moment arrives.
パンサーは、その時が来るまで待ち伏せしています

This is the patience of predators who hunt to survive.
これは生き残るために狩りをする捕食者の忍耐力です

That same patience burned inside Buck as he stayed close.
バックが近くにいる間、同じ忍耐が彼の心の中で燃え上がった

He stayed near the herd, slowing its march and stirring fear.
彼は群れの近くに留まり、群れの行進を遅らせ、恐怖をかき立てた

He teased the young bulls and harassed the mother cows.
彼は若い雄牛をいじめ、母牛を困らせた

He drove the wounded bull into a deeper, helpless rage.
彼は傷ついた雄牛をさらに深い、無力な怒りに追い込んだ

For half a day, the fight dragged on with no rest at all.
戦いは半日の間、休むことなく続いた

Buck attacked from every angle, fast and fierce as wind.
バックは風のように速く激しく、あらゆる角度から攻撃しました

He kept the bull from resting or hiding with its herd.
彼は雄牛が群れと一緒に休んだり隠れたりしないようにした

Buck wore down the moose's will faster than its body.
雄鹿はヘラジカの体よりも早くその意志を弱らせた

The day passed and the sun sank low in the northwest sky.
日が暮れて、太陽は北西の空に沈んでいった

The young bulls returned more slowly to help their leader.
若い雄牛たちはリーダーを助けるためにゆっくりと戻ってきました

Fall nights had returned, and darkness now lasted six hours.
秋の夜が戻ってきて、暗闇が6時間続きました

Winter was pressing them downhill into safer, warmer valleys.
冬は彼らをより安全で暖かい谷へと追いやっていた

But still they couldn't escape the hunter that held them back.
しかし、それでも彼らは彼らを阻止していたハンターから逃げることはできませんでした

Only one life was at stake—not the herd's, just their leader's.
危険にさらされているのは、群れの命ではなく、リーダーの命だけだった

That made the threat distant and not their urgent concern.
これにより、脅威は遠いものとなり、彼らにとって差し迫った懸念ではなくなった

In time, they accepted this cost and let Buck take the old bull.
やがて彼らはこの代償を受け入れ、バックに老雄牛を連れて行くことを許可した

As twilight settled in, the old bull stood with his head down.
夕暮れが訪れると、年老いた雄牛は頭を下げて立っていた

He watched the herd he had led vanish into the fading light.
彼は自分が率いていた群れが薄れゆく光の中に消えていくのを見守った

There were cows he had known, calves he had once fathered.
そこには彼が知っていた牛たち、かつて彼が父親にした子牛たちもいた

There were younger bulls he had fought and ruled in past seasons.
過去のシーズンでは、彼が闘い、勝利した若い雄牛たちもいた

He could not follow them—for before him crouched Buck again.

彼は彼らについていくことができなかったなぜなら彼の前にバックが再びうずくまっていたからだ

The merciless fanged terror blocked every path he might take.

容赦ない牙を持った恐怖が、彼が進むべき道をすべて塞いだ

The bull weighed more than three hundredweight of dense power.

その雄牛は三百ポンド以上の重さがあり、濃厚な力を持っていた

He had lived long and fought hard in a world of struggle.

彼は長く生き、闘争の世界で懸命に戦った

Yet now, at the end, death came from a beast far beneath him.

しかし今、最後には、彼のはるか下にいる獣から死がもたらされた

Buck's head did not even rise to the bull's huge knuckled knees.

バックの頭は雄牛の巨大な関節のある膝まで届きませんでした

From that moment on, Buck stayed with the bull night and day.

その瞬間から、バックは昼も夜も雄牛と一緒にいた

He never gave him rest, never allowed him to graze or drink.

彼は決して彼に休息を与えず、草を食べたり水を飲むことも許さなかった

The bull tried to eat young birch shoots and willow leaves.

雄牛は若い白樺の芽と柳の葉を食べようとしました

But Buck drove him off, always alert and always attacking.

しかしバックは常に警戒し、攻撃しながら彼を追い払いました

Even at trickling streams, Buck blocked every thirsty attempt.

細流であっても、バックは喉が渇いた者のあらゆる試み
を阻止した

Sometimes, in desperation, the bull fled at full speed.
時には、絶望のあまり、雄牛は全速力で逃げることもあ
った

Buck let him run, loping calmly just behind, never far away.
バックは彼を走らせ、決して遠く離れることなく、すぐ
後ろを静かに走り続けた

When the moose paused, Buck lay down, but stayed ready.
ヘラジカが立ち止まると、バックは横たわりましたが、
準備は整っていました

If the bull tried to eat or drink, Buck struck with full fury.
雄牛が食べたり飲んだりしようとすると、雄牛は激怒し
て攻撃した

The bull's great head sagged lower under its vast antlers.
雄牛の大きな頭は、その巨大な角の下に垂れ下がってい
た

His pace slowed, the trot became a heavy; a stumbling walk.
彼の歩調は遅くなり、小走りは重くなり、よろめきなが
ら歩くようになった

He often stood still with drooped ears and nose to the
ground.
彼はよく耳を垂らし、鼻を地面につけてじっと立ってい
ました

During those moments, Buck took time to drink and rest.
その間、バックは水を飲んだり休んだりする時間を取っ
た

Tongue out, eyes fixed, Buck sensed the land was changing.
舌を出し、目を凝らして、バックは土地が変化している
ことを感じ取った

He felt something new moving through the forest and sky.
彼は森と空を何か新しいものが動いているのを感じた

As moose returned, so did other creatures of the wild.
ヘラジカが戻ってくると、他の野生の生き物たちも戻っ
てきました

The land felt alive with presence, unseen but strongly known.

その土地は、目に見えないけれども、強く知られている存在で生き生きしているように感じました

It was not by sound, sight, nor by scent that Buck knew this.

バックがそれを知ったのは、音でも視覚でも嗅覚でもなかった

A deeper sense told him that new forces were on the move.

より深い感覚が彼に、新たな勢力が動き出していると告げた

Strange life stirred through the woods and along the streams.

森の中や小川沿いに奇妙な生命が動き回っていました

He resolved to explore this spirit, after the hunt was complete.

彼は狩りが終わった後、この精霊を探索しようと決心した

On the fourth day, Buck brought down the moose at last.

4日目に、バックはついにヘラジカを倒しました

He stayed by the kill for a full day and night, feeding and resting.

彼は獲物のそばに丸一日と一晩留まり、餌を食べたり休んだりした

He ate, then slept, then ate again, until he was strong and full.

彼は食べて、寝て、また食べて、満腹になって元気になるまで続けました

When he was ready, he turned back toward camp and Thornton.

準備が整うと、彼はキャンプとソーントンの方へ引き返した

With steady pace, he began the long return journey home.

彼は一定のペースで長い帰路に着いた

He ran in his tireless lope, hour after hour, never once straying.

彼は疲れを知らない速歩で何時間も走り続け、一度も道に迷うことはなかった

Through unknown lands, he moved straight as a compass needle.

未知の土地を、彼はコンパスの針のようにまっすぐに進んだ

His sense of direction made man and map seem weak by comparison.

それに比べると、彼の方向感覚は人間や地図よりも弱いように思えた

As Buck ran, he felt more strongly the stir in the wild land.

バックが走っていると、荒野のざわめきがさらに強く感じられるようになった

It was a new kind of life, unlike that of the calm summer months.

それは穏やかな夏の数ヶ月の生活とは異なる、新しい種類の生活でした

This feeling no longer came as a subtle or distant message.

この気持ちはもはや微妙な、あるいは遠いメッセージとして伝わってきませんでした

Now the birds spoke of this life, and squirrels chattered about it.

今、鳥たちはこの人生について語り、リスたちはそれについておしゃべりしていました

Even the breeze whispered warnings through the silent trees.

静かな木々の間からそよ風が警告をささやきさえも伝えた

Several times he stopped and sniffed the fresh morning air.

彼は何度か立ち止まって、新鮮な朝の空気を吸い込んだ

He read a message there that made him leap forward faster.

彼はそこでメッセージを読み、さらに速く前進した

A heavy sense of danger filled him, as if something had gone wrong.

まるで何かが間違っていたかのように、彼は強い危険感に襲われた

He feared calamity was coming—or had already come.
彼は災難が来ることを恐れた――あるいはすでに来てしまったのだ

He crossed the last ridge and entered the valley below.
彼は最後の尾根を越えて下の谷に入った

He moved more slowly, alert and cautious with every step.
彼は一歩ごとに注意深く、慎重にゆっくりと動いた

Three miles out he found a fresh trail that made him stiffen.
3マイルほど進んだところで、彼は新しい道を見つけ、体が固くなった

The hair along his neck rippled and bristled in alarm.
彼の首の毛は驚きで波立ち、逆立った

The trail led straight toward the camp where Thornton waited.
その道はソーントンが待つキャンプへとまっすぐ続いていた

Buck moved faster now, his stride both silent and swift.
バックはより速く動いたその歩調は静かで素早かった

His nerves tightened as he read signs others were going to miss.
他の人が見逃しそうな兆候を読み取り、彼の神経は張り詰めた

Each detail in the trail told a story—except the final piece.
道のそれぞれの細部が物語を語っていたが、最後の部分だけはそうではなかった

His nose told him about the life that had passed this way.
彼の鼻は、この道を通ってきた人生について語っていた

The scent gave him a changing picture as he followed close behind.
彼がすぐ後ろをついていくと、匂いによって変化する光景が目に浮かびました

But the forest itself had gone quiet; unnaturally still.
しかし、森そのものは不自然なほど静かになっていました

Birds had vanished, squirrels were hidden, silent and still.

鳥は姿を消し、リスは隠れて、静かに動かなくなっていた

He saw only one gray squirrel, flat on a dead tree.
彼は枯れ木の上に平らに寝ている灰色のリスを一匹だけ見た

The squirrel blended in, stiff and motionless like a part of the forest.
リスは森の一部のように硬直して動かず、溶け込んでいました

Buck moved like a shadow, silent and sure through the trees.
バックは木々の間を静かに、そして確実に影のように動いた

His nose jerked sideways as if pulled by an unseen hand.
彼の鼻は、まるで見えない手に引っ張られたかのように横に動いた

He turned and followed the new scent deep into a thicket.
彼は向きを変え、新たな匂いを追って茂みの奥深くへと入った

There he found Nig, lying dead, pierced through by an arrow.
そこで彼は、矢に刺されて死んで横たわっているニグを発見した

The shaft passed clear through his body, feathers still showing.
矢は彼の体を貫通したが、羽はまだ見えていた

Nig had dragged himself there, but died before reaching help.
ニグさんはそこまで這って来たが、助けが来る前に亡くなった

A hundred yards farther on, Buck found another sled dog.
さらに100ヤードほど進むと、バックはもう一匹のそり犬を見つけた

It was a dog that Thornton had bought back in Dawson City.
それはソーントンがドーソン・シティで買った犬だった

The dog was in a death struggle, thrashing hard on the trail.
犬は道の上で激しく暴れながら、必死にもがいていた

Buck passed around him, not stopping, eyes fixed ahead.
バックは立ち止まることなく、前を見つめながら彼の周りを通り過ぎた

From the direction of the camp came a distant, rhythmic chant.
キャンプの方向から遠くからリズミカルな詠唱が聞こえてきた

Voices rose and fell in a strange, eerie, sing-song tone.
声は奇妙で不気味な、歌うような調子で上がったり下がったりした

Buck crawled forward to the edge of the clearing in silence.
バックは黙って空き地の端まで這っていった

There he saw Hans lying face-down, pierced with many arrows.
そこで彼は、ハンスが多数の矢に刺されてうつ伏せになっているのを見ました

His body looked like a porcupine, bristling with feathered shafts.
彼の体は、羽毛のついた毛が密生したヤマアラシのようだった

At the same moment, Buck looked toward the ruined lodge.
同時に、バックは廃墟となったロッジの方へ目を向けた

The sight made the hair rise stiff on his neck and shoulders.
その光景を見て、彼の首と肩の毛が逆立った

A storm of wild rage swept through Buck's whole body.
激しい怒りの嵐がバックの全身を襲った

He growled aloud, though he did not know that he had.
彼は大声でうなったが、自分がそうしていたことには気づいていなかった

The sound was raw, filled with terrifying, savage fury.
その音は生々しく、恐ろしく野蛮な怒りに満ちていた

For the last time in his life, Buck lost reason to emotion.
バックは生涯で最後に、感情に理性を失った

It was love for John Thornton that broke his careful control.
彼の慎重な制御を破ったのは、ジョン・ソーントンへの愛だった

The Yeehats were dancing around the wrecked spruce lodge.
イェーハット族は破壊されたトウヒ材のロッジの周りで踊っていました

Then came a roar—and an unknown beast charged toward them.
すると、轟音が響き、正体不明の獣が彼らに向かって突進してきた

It was Buck; a fury in motion; a living storm of vengeance.
それはバックだった動き出した激怒、生きた復讐の嵐だった

He flung himself into their midst, mad with the need to kill.
彼は殺人への欲求に狂い、彼らの真ん中に飛び込んだ

He leapt at the first man, the Yeehat chief, and struck true.
彼は最初の男、イーハット族の族長に飛びかかり、真正面から攻撃した

His throat was ripped open, and blood spouted in a stream.
彼の喉は裂け、血が流れ出た

Buck did not stop, but tore the next man's throat with one leap.
バックは止まらず、一跳びで次の男の喉を引き裂いた

He was unstoppable—ripping, slashing, never pausing to rest.
彼は止められない存在だった引き裂き、斬りつけ、決して休む暇もなかった

He darted and sprang so fast their arrows could not touch him.
彼は非常に速く突進し、跳躍したので、矢は彼に届かなかった

The Yeehats were caught in their own panic and confusion.
イェーハット族はパニックと混乱に陥っていた

Their arrows missed Buck and struck one another instead.
彼らの矢はバックを外れ、代わりに互いの矢に当たった

One youth threw a spear at Buck and hit another man.
一人の若者がバックに槍を投げ、別の男を襲った

The spear drove through his chest, the point punching out his back.

槍は彼の胸を貫き、槍の先端は彼の背中を突き破った

Terror swept over the Yeehats, and they broke into full retreat.

恐怖がイーハット族を襲い、彼らは全面撤退を余儀なくされた

They screamed of the Evil Spirit and fled into the forest shadows.

彼らは悪霊に叫びながら森の影の中へ逃げました

Truly, Buck was like a demon as he chased the Yeehats down.

本当に、バックはイーハットを追いかけるとき、まるで悪魔のようでした

He tore after them through the forest, bringing them down like deer.

彼は森の中を彼らを追いかけ、鹿のように倒した

It became a day of fate and terror for the frightened Yeehats.

怯えたイーハッツにとって、それは運命と恐怖の日となった

They scattered across the land, fleeing far in every direction.

彼らは国中に散らばり、四方八方遠くまで逃げていった

A full week passed before the last survivors met in a valley.

最後の生存者が谷間で出会うまでに丸一週間が経過した

Only then did they count their losses and speak of what happened.

そのとき初めて、彼らは損失を計算し、何が起こったかを語りました

Buck, after tiring of the chase, returned to the ruined camp.

バックは追跡に疲れて、破壊されたキャンプに戻った

He found Pete, still in his blankets, killed in the first attack.

彼は、最初の攻撃で殺されたピートがまだ毛布にくるまっていたのを発見した

Signs of Thornton's last struggle were marked in the dirt nearby.

近くの土にはソーントンの最後の闘いの跡が残っていた

Buck followed every trace, sniffing each mark to a final point.

バックはあらゆる痕跡をたどり、それぞれの痕跡を嗅ぎながら最終地点に到達した

At the edge of a deep pool, he found faithful Skeet, lying still.

深い池の端で、彼は忠実なスキートがじっと横たわっているのを見つけた

Skeet's head and front paws were in the water, unmoving in death.

スキートの頭と前足は水中にあり、死んで動かなかった

The pool was muddy and tainted with runoff from the sluice boxes.

プールは水門からの流出水で泥だらけになって汚れていた

Its cloudy surface hid what lay beneath, but Buck knew the truth.

曇った表面の下に何があるのかは隠されていたが、バックは真実を知っていた

He tracked Thornton's scent into the pool — but the scent led nowhere else.

彼はソーントンの匂いをプールまで追跡したが、その匂いはどこにも通じていなかった

There was no scent leading out — only the silence of deep water.

外に通じる匂いはなく、ただ深い水の静寂だけが残っていた

All day Buck stayed near the pool, pacing the camp in grief.

バックは一日中池の近くにいて、悲しみに暮れながらキャンプ場を歩き回っていた

He wandered restlessly or sat in stillness, lost in heavy thought.

彼は落ち着きなく歩き回ったり、じっと座って深い考えにふけったりしていた

He knew death; the ending of life; the vanishing of all motion.

彼は死を知っていた人生の終わりを知っていたすべての動きが消え去ることも知っていた

He understood that John Thornton was gone, never to return.

彼はジョン・ソーントンはもう戻ってこないことを理解した

The loss left an empty space in him that throbbed like hunger.

その喪失は彼の中に飢えのように脈打つ空虚感を残した

But this was a hunger food could not ease, no matter how much he ate.

しかし、これは、どれだけ食べても和らぐことのない空腹感でした

At times, as he looked at the dead Yeehats, the pain faded.

時折、死んだイーハットたちを見ていると、痛みは消えていった

And then a strange pride rose inside him, fierce and complete.

そして、彼の中に、激しく、完全な奇妙な誇りが湧き上がった

He had killed man, the highest and most dangerous game of all.

彼は人間を殺したそれはあらゆるゲームの中で最も高尚で危険な行為だった

He had killed in defiance of the ancient law of club and fang.

彼は棍棒と牙を使った古代の法に反して殺人を犯した

Buck sniffed their lifeless bodies, curious and thoughtful.

バックは好奇心と思慮深さをもって、彼らの死んだ体を嗅ぎました

They had died so easily—much easier than a husky in a fight.

彼らはとても簡単に死んだ喧嘩中のハスキー犬よりもずっと簡単に

Without their weapons, they had no true strength or threat.

武器がなければ、彼らには真の力も脅威もなかった

Buck was never going to fear them again, unless they were armed.

彼らが武装していない限り、バックは彼らを二度と恐れるつもりはなかった

Only when they carried clubs, spears, or arrows he'd beware.
彼らが棍棒、槍、または矢を持っているときだけ、彼は警戒した

Night fell, and a full moon rose high above the tops of the trees.
夜が来て、満月が木々の梢の上に高く昇りました

The moon's pale light bathed the land in a soft, ghostly glow like day.
月の淡い光が、昼間のように柔らかく幽霊のような輝きで大地を照らしていた

As the night deepened, Buck still mourned by the silent pool.
夜が更けるにつれ、バックは静かな池のそばでまだ悲しみに暮れていた

Then he became aware of a different stirring in the forest.
そのとき、彼は森の中で何かが異様に動いていることに気づいた

The stirring was not from the Yeehats, but from something older and deeper.
その動揺はイーハット族からではなく、もっと古くてもっと深いところから来たものだった

He stood up, ears lifted, nose testing the breeze with care.
彼は立ち上がり、耳を上げ、鼻で風を注意深く確かめた

From far away came a faint, sharp yelp that pierced the silence.
遠くからかすかに鋭い叫び声が聞こえ、静寂を破った

Then a chorus of similar cries followed close behind the first.
それから、最初の叫び声のすぐ後に、同じような叫び声が次々と続いた

The sound drew nearer, growing louder with each passing moment.
その音は刻一刻と大きくなり、近づいてきた

Buck knew this cry—it came from that other world in his memory.

バックはこの叫びを知っていた——それは彼の記憶の中の別の世界から来たものだった

He walked to the center of the open space and listened closely.

彼は広場の中央まで歩いていき、耳を澄ませた

The call rang out, many-noted and more powerful than ever.

その呼びかけは多くの人に届き、これまで以上に力強く響き渡りました

And now, more than ever before, Buck was ready to answer his calling.

そして今、これまで以上に、バックは彼の呼びかけに応える準備ができていた

John Thornton was dead, and no tie to man remained within him.

ジョン・ソーントンは亡くなり、彼の中には人間との絆は残っていなかった

Man and all human claims were gone—he was free at last.

人間とすべての人間の権利は消え去り、ついに彼は自由になった

The wolf pack were chasing meat like the Yeehats once had.

オオカミの群れは、かつてイーハット族がやっていたように肉を追い求めていた

They had followed moose down from the timbered lands.

彼らは森林地帯からヘラジカを追って降りてきた

Now, wild and hungry for prey, they crossed into his valley.

今、彼らは野生化し、獲物に飢え、彼の谷へと侵入した

Into the moonlit clearing they came, flowing like silver water.

彼らは、銀色の水のように流れながら、月明かりに照らされた空き地に入ってきた

Buck stood still in the center, motionless and waiting for them.

バックは中央でじっと立ち、動かずに彼らを待っていた

His calm, large presence stunned the pack into a brief silence.

彼の穏やかで大きな存在感は、群衆を驚かせ、しばしの沈黙をもたらした

Then the boldest wolf leapt straight at him without hesitation.

すると、最も大胆なオオカミがためらうことなくまっすぐに彼に飛びかかりました

Buck struck fast and broke the wolf's neck in a single blow.

バックは素早く攻撃し、一撃でオオカミの首を折った

He stood motionless again as the dying wolf twisted behind him.

死にゆく狼が背後で身をよじる中、彼は再び動かずに立っていた

Three more wolves attacked quickly, one after the other.

さらに3匹のオオカミが次々に素早く攻撃してきました

Each retreated bleeding, their throats or shoulders slashed.

喉や肩を切り裂かれ、血を流しながら退却した

That was enough to trigger the whole pack into a wild charge.

それは群れ全体を狂暴に突撃させるには十分だった

They rushed in together, too eager and crowded to strike well.

彼らは一斉に突進したが、あまりに熱心で密集していたため、うまく攻撃することができなかった

Buck's speed and skill allowed him to stay ahead of the attack.

バックのスピードと技術により、彼は攻撃を先取りすることができた

He spun on his hind legs, snapping and striking in all directions.

彼は後ろ足で回転し、あらゆる方向に音を立てて攻撃した

To the wolves, this seemed like his defense never opened or faltered.

オオカミたちにとって、彼の守備は決して開いたり、弱まったりしなかったように思えた

He turned and slashed so quickly they could not get behind him.

彼は向きを変えて素早く斬りつけたので、敵は彼の背後に回り込むことができなかった

Nonetheless, their numbers forced him to give ground and fall back.

それにもかかわらず、敵の数の多さから、彼は屈服し、後退せざるを得なかった

He moved past the pool and down into the rocky creek bed.

彼は池を通り過ぎ、岩だらけの川底へと降りていった

There he came up against a steep bank of gravel and dirt.

そこで彼は砂利と土の急な土手にぶつかった

He edged into a corner cut during the miners' old digging.

彼は、鉱夫たちが昔採掘していたときに切り開かれた角に滑り込んだ

Now, protected on three sides, Buck faced only the front wolf.

今、バックは三方から守られ、前にいるオオカミとだけ対峙していた

There, he stood at bay, ready for the next wave of assault.

そこで彼は、次の攻撃の波に備えて、立ち止まっていた

Buck held his ground so fiercely that the wolves drew back.

バックは猛烈に抵抗したので、オオカミたちは後ずさりした

After half an hour, they were worn out and visibly defeated.

30 分後、彼らは疲れ果て、明らかに敗北していた

Their tongues hung out, their white fangs gleamed in moonlight.

彼らの舌は突き出ており、白い牙は月の光に輝いていた

Some wolves lay down, heads raised, ears pricked toward Buck.

何匹かのオオカミが頭を上げ、耳をバックのほうに向けて横たわっていた

Others stood still, alert and watching his every move.

他の人たちはじっと立って、警戒しながら彼の一挙手一投足を見守っていた

A few wandered to the pool and lapped up cold water.
数人がプールまで歩いて行き、冷たい水を飲みました

Then one long, lean gray wolf crept forward in a gentle way.
すると、一匹の細長い灰色のオオカミが、静かに前に進み出てきました

Buck recognized him—it was the wild brother from before.
バックは彼に気づいた——それは先ほどの荒々しい兄弟だった

The gray wolf whined softly, and Buck replied with a whine.
灰色のオオカミが小さく鳴くと、バックも鳴き返した

They touched noses, quietly and without threat or fear.
彼らは静かに、脅したり恐れたりすることなく、鼻を合わせた

Next came an older wolf, gaunt and scarred from many battles.
次にやってきたのは、多くの戦いでやつれ傷を負った年老いた狼だった

Buck started to snarl, but paused and sniffed the old wolf's nose.
バックはうなり声を上げ始めたが、立ち止まって老いたオオカミの鼻を嗅いだ

The old one sat down, raised his nose, and howled at the moon.
老人は座り、鼻を上げて、月に向かって吠えました

The rest of the pack sat down and joined in the long howl.
群れの残りも座り込み、長い遠吠えに加わった

And now the call came to Buck, unmistakable and strong.
そして今、その呼びかけは、紛れもなく力強い声でバックに届いた

He sat down, lifted his head, and howled with the others.
彼は座り、頭を上げて、他の者たちと一緒に遠吠えしました

When the howling ended, Buck stepped out of his rocky shelter.

遠吠えが止むと、バックは岩陰から出てきました

The pack closed in around him, sniffing both kindly and warily.

群れは優しくも警戒しながらも彼を取り囲んだ

Then the leaders gave the yelp and dashed off into the forest.

するとリーダーたちは叫び声をあげて森の中へ駆け出して行きました

The other wolves followed, yelping in chorus, wild and fast in the night.

他のオオカミたちもそれに続き、夜に激しく速く合唱して吠えた

Buck ran with them, beside his wild brother, howling as he ran.

バックは野生児の兄弟の横で彼らと一緒に走り、走りながら吠えた

Here, the story of Buck does well to come to its end.

ここで、バックの物語はうまく終わりを迎えます

In the years that followed, the Yeehats noticed strange wolves.

その後の数年間、イーハット家は奇妙なオオカミの存在に気づいた

Some had brown on their heads and muzzles, white on the chest.

中には頭と鼻先が茶色で、胸が白いものもいた

But even more, they feared a ghostly figure among the wolves.

しかし、彼らはさらに、オオカミの中に幽霊のような人物がいることを恐れていた

They spoke in whispers of the Ghost Dog, leader of the pack.

彼らは群れのリーダーであるゴーストドッグについてささやきながら話した

This Ghost Dog had more cunning than the boldest Yeehat hunter.

このゴースト ドッグは、最も大胆な Yeehat ハンターよりも狡猾でした

The ghost dog stole from camps in deep winter and tore their traps apart.

幽霊犬は真冬にキャンプから盗みを働き、罠を破壊した

The ghost dog killed their dogs and escaped their arrows without a trace.

幽霊犬は彼らの犬を殺し、跡形もなく彼らの矢から逃れました

Even their bravest warriors feared to face this wild spirit.

最も勇敢な戦士たちでさえ、この荒々しい霊に立ち向かうことを恐れた

No, the tale grows darker still, as the years pass in the wild.

いいえ、荒野で年月が経つにつれ、物語はさらに暗くなっていきます

Some hunters vanish and never return to their distant camps.

ハンターの中には姿を消し、遠くのキャンプに二度と戻らない者もいる

Others are found with their throats torn open, slain in the snow.

喉を引き裂かれ、雪の中で殺害された状態で発見される者もいる

Around their bodies are tracks—larger than any wolf could make.

彼らの体の周りには、どんなオオカミでもつけられないほど大きな足跡があります

Each autumn, Yeehats follow the trail of the moose.

毎年秋になると、イーハット族はヘラジカの足跡をたどります

But they avoid one valley with fear carved deep into their hearts.

しかし、彼らは心の奥底に恐怖を刻み込み、ある谷を避けている

They say the valley is chosen by the Evil Spirit for his home.

この谷は悪霊の住処として選ばれたと言われています

And when the tale is told, some women weep beside the fire.

そして、その物語が語られると、何人かの女性は火のそばで泣きます

But in summer, one visitor comes to that quiet, sacred valley.

しかし夏になると、その静かで神聖な谷に一人の訪問者がやって来ます

The Yeehats do not know of him, nor could they understand.

イェハット族は彼のことを知らず、理解することもできなかった

The wolf is a great one, coated in glory, like no other of his kind.

オオカミは、同種の他のどの動物とも違って、栄光に覆われた偉大な存在です

He alone crosses from green timber and enters the forest glade.

彼は一人で緑の木々の間を渡り、森の空き地へと入っていった

There, golden dust from moose-hide sacks seeps into the soil.

そこでは、ヘラジカの皮の袋から出た金色の粉が土に染み込んでいます

Grass and old leaves have hidden the yellow from the sun.

草や古い葉が太陽からの黄色を隠しています

Here, the wolf stands in silence, thinking and remembering.

ここで、オオカミは静かに立ち、考え、思い出しています

He howls once—long and mournful—before he turns to go.

彼は立ち去る前に、一度長く悲しげな遠吠えをしました

Yet he is not always alone in the land of cold and snow.

しかし、寒さと雪の国では彼はいつも一人ぼっちというわけではない

When long winter nights descend on the lower valleys.

長い冬の夜が谷底に降り注ぐとき

When the wolves follow game through moonlight and frost.
オオカミが月明かりと霜の中、獲物を追うとき
Then he runs at the head of the pack, leaping high and wild.
それから彼は群れの先頭に立ち、高く激しくジャンプし
ながら走ります
His shape towers over the others, his throat alive with song.
彼の姿は他の者たちよりも高くそびえ立ち、喉には歌声
が響いている
It is the song of the younger world, the voice of the pack.
それは若い世界の歌であり、群れの声です
He sings as he runs—strong, free, and forever wild.
彼は走りながら歌う力強く、自由に、そして永遠に野性
的

www.ingramcontent.com/pod-product-compliance
Lightning Source LLC
Chambersburg PA
CBHW011730020426
42333CB00024B/2822